To
Lenya & Luca Joe

#1
Cowgirl
Chryle 2014

The Diary of
MISS WILD WEST
A True Story

© Copyright 2013 by Chyrle Bacon

ISBN - 978-1-4675-9495-0

Published by: Chyrle Bacon

Printed in the United States

For all general information online : www.cowgirlchyrle.com

To contact Chyrle via e-mail: ropepro@yahoo.com

Non-fictional story.

DEDICATION

I want to dedicate this book to all those young cowboys and cowgirls who dream of someday making it big. Have confidence in yourselves, and you may earn that big break.

Just follow your dreams!

ACKNOWLEDGEMENTS

First and foremost, my thanks to Montie Montana, Jr., who "discovered" me. I wouldn't be entertaining folks (and loving it!) if he hadn't sauntered into the bank that particular day...

To John Brady, the amazing Australian boomerang thrower, trick roper, and whip artist, who graciously shared some of his trick roping and whip skill sets with me, so I can entertain folks today.

To Vi Brady, a beautiful lady who had so much class! I continue to thank her in my mind and heart for her being my mentor, a perfect example in bearing and dress, and my confidante. She was one special lady who fully believed in me!

To Cathy Fuller, my editor who helped me with the writing of this story.

To Bruce Brennen, whose magic touch and skill created these fantastic free hand sketches and cover picture oil painting.

And thanks to all those Western performers I have met along the way. Together we can still "wow" the audiences.

Chyrle Bacon,
"Miss Wild West"

THE AUTHOR

As a "Miss Wild West", Chyrle Bacon, a statuesque, blonde beauty, travels internationally sharing her multitalented charm with wide-ranging audiences. She creates a sizzling, exciting and dynamic atmosphere wherever she performs. Her shows have thrilled crowds as large as 70,000 or as small as a backyard BBQ.

Being very proud of her heritage, Chyrle says, "I owe my spirit and personality to my ancestors. My Great-Grandmother was Princess Rose, a Cherokee princess. And if my Aunt Jo's love had a different twist of fate, I would be related to Wild Bill Cody." Chyrle claims it is the Cherokee blood that flows in her veins that drives her ambitions and desire to entertain and delight those around her.

As both a performer and a producer, she applies her multi-talents and exciting roping tricks as well as whip cracking to thrill audiences. In addition to local shows, Chyrle's background as a spokesperson in Public Relations is beneficial when promoting these shows with press, radio and TV reporters.

THE HEADLINE ACT

- Buffalo Bill's Wild West Show | US & World Tour
- Knott's Berry Farm | CA
- Reno Hilton Theater backed by the Philharmonic Orchestra
- Rawhide Park | AZ
- Frontier Village | San Jose, CA
- Coyote Ranch | Coyote, CA
- Great America Park | Santa Clara, CA
- Marine World / Africa USA | CA
- East/West Shriner Football Game
- Los Angeles Rams Football Game Half-Time Shows
- San Francisco. 49ers Football Game Half-Time Shows
- Hawaii Pro-Bowl Football Game Half-Time Show
- Long Branch Saloon and Farms | Half Moon Bay, CA

AWARDS

- 1993 Guinness Book of World Records for Largest Loop Spun | Woman's Division
- 1994 "Western Performer of the Year" International Cowboy & Indian Congress | Scottsdale, AZ
- 1995 to 1997 Titled "Miss Lone Star" from visits to China
- 1995 & 1998 "Showmanship Award Trophy" | Las Vegas, Nevada

Montie Montana Jr.

Ring: (559) 539-3500
Fax: (559) 539-3836
Email: mm@buffalobill.com
URL: http://www.buffalobill.com

P.O. Box 1060
Springville, California 93265-1060 USA

To Whom It May Concern

Howdy!

Chyrle Bacon has served as "Miss Wild West" for the Buffalo Bill Wild West Show on a number of overseas tours and appearances in the United States. Overseas included, Malaysia, Singapore, Japan, Brazil, Germany and others, and most recently in Oregon.

Chyrle has developed a number of performing skills, working with the top Wild ™ West attractions, and during her career has many memories to share with her readers. She is the one and only "Miss Wild West" and we wish her the best.

Sincerely,

Montie Montana Jr.
Buffalo Bill's Wild West
PO Box 1060
Springville, CA 93265

Bruce Brannen, Illustrator

Table of Contents

Chapter 1

Unexpected Options

Friday was just another routine day at the bank as a teller. Another tedious, colorless workday at a job that seemed to make days blend together. My dream was to travel the world, but I found myself doing the daily tasks of waking up, dressing for work, going to work, and then coming back to my apartment. The only activity that changed was the weekly grocery shopping. But as luck had it, my life was about to change. To give you an idea of my past, I will take you back a few years.

Except for a few of my early years in Iowa, I grew up in Escondido, California - which is north of San Diego - in a middle-class community. I went to grade and high school near my parent's home. My father and mother both worked extremely hard to make all the bills that come with owning a home. Since I was an only child and my mother was away from the house all day, I was expected to help around the house, doing housework and fixing dinner after I got home from school each day. My father pushed me to become a successful businesswoman, with a college degree. But that was not where my heart was!

During my junior year of high school, I joined classes in Hawaiian dancing, then in my senior year I entered the "Miss Escondido" beauty contest where I got as far as the fifth runner-up. My parents supported me in my Hawaiian classes – my dad had a beautiful singing voice and he would sing as I danced at dance class or special occasioned luaus, but he was not happy about my modeling or entering a beauty contest! He wanted me to have a secure life with a secure job. I thought "Boring!!" I want to travel! After high school, I commuted a few miles to Palomar Community College to take courses in business machines. While I was in college, I moved in with a friend and we supported our rent expenses with part time jobs. I also began modeling classes – since I was so tall and kept hearing from friends and my parents' friends how pretty I was and "why aren't you a model?" Not to brag, but as a tall, willowy brunette with golden highlights in her hair, I was (and was told) a real shapely beauty.

After a year and a half at a community college, I applied for a flight attendant's job with United Airlines. I had always wanted to see the world – this was an unfulfilled dream! But, all airlines had a height requirement and I was refused because I was too tall (I am 5'11"). Such a disappointment! I was so hoping to get this job!

My next thought was to apply for a modeling job as I had now graduated from modeling school. Surely there would be travel opportunities with this position! Another girlfriend and I decided to move closer to Los Angeles where modeling jobs were more plentiful. We split the difference in distances by finding a place in Newport Beach (which is about thirty miles from downtown Los Angeles).

Both the Balboa Bay Club and Newport Inn Country Club in Newport Beach, California, had fashion shows for afternoon women's luncheons and needed models. I applied and was hired for both jobs. I was so excited! Working at the Balboa Bay Club was really interesting as you would never know who you might see. I was able to meet several movie stars. While stopping by the Balboa Bay Club on an errand one evening, I noticed a huge gathering. John Wayne (long time actor of westerns and action movies, American Legend and folk hero) was one of those in this group. He was so tall, handsome, strong, and charismatic with a very deep voice! I was able to gather my courage to join his small band of friends, walking to the right side of Mr. Wayne, where I nervously

began my conversation by introducing myself. He quickly noticed my tall stature (he was a very tall man himself), inquiring politely about my height. During our short conversation, he was extremely gracious to speak with me, being we had never formally met before this moment! This was exciting to me, since I'd always been a fan of his and enjoyed the western movies he starred in.

Modeling jobs were sporadic, at best, and the pay wasn't enough for me to live on, even with a roommate who shared all of the expenses. Still, another job was needed for more income, so I began looking through the newspapers. I came across one that I thought would be right for me – a teller position at a bank (since I had taken all those business classes in college). I was sure I could work full time and keep my modeling job too, since the bank (teller) position hours were during the day and modeling was during the evening and weekends. When I made the call, a person at the bank set up an interview for the next day.

I was really nervous at my job interview, so I took a deep breath to calm down. Twenty minutes later, the job was mine (plus I would begin training the next day)! I spent the rest of the day getting my wardrobe together for my new job. I had never worked in a bank before, so I felt apprehensive. The idea of handling other peoples' money and making sure that my money drawer was correct at the end of the day concerned me greatly.

When I showed up at eight o'clock am for work, I realized this was going to be a long day. At first I was enthusiastic and comfortable about my duties since I was only observing others at their job, then came my turn to work with customers and their money. Mrs. Mason, my supervisor, was a matronly, no-nonsense type woman with salt-and-pepper colored hair. She insisted that every procedure was followed with precision and completed accurately, so she noted my actions carefully as I greeted my first customer. Mrs. Mason's presence added stress to this moment since I was not yet confident on how to log money transactions. I did eventually figure out all the proper procedures of deposits and withdrawals for customers. When I got home from work, I felt drained emotionally and physically. I ate dinner and went straight to bed.

After about a week, I felt accepted by my fellow workers, becoming familiar with my 'regular' customers and, most importantly, my cash drawer always balanced to the penny! I finally figured out that it took more than exactness and precision to be an excellent teller; it also took having a warm personality, a friendly smile, an honest disposition and learning to have faith in oneself.

Moving was now a necessity. Since my present roommate was leaving, and I could not afford the rent alone, Saturday I bought a newspaper in which I found a wonderful place to live on Balboa Island. Now this two-bedroom upstairs apartment was steps from the bay and beach - a fantastic view that overlooked the peninsula - a dream come true! This location was also in an upscale part of town. But, I needed a roommate to share the rent. What to do?! A couple of days after my current roommate had informed me of her leaving, I was in the lunchroom at the bank where I met a girl named Judy. She worked in accounts-payable which was in a different area within the bank than my teller area. We chatted for a bit and during the course of our visit over lunch; I discovered she was looking for a roommate as well! She and I eagerly joined forces so we could rent this super apartment!

Judy had blonde hair, blue eyes and was very shapely, and she sure did like to party! She also had no end of party-loving friends. One night while Judy was entertaining, I heard my bedroom door open just before I dozed off to sleep. Standing at my now-opened door was one of Judy's guy-friends, visiting for the evening. At first I thought this fellow was very confused and just looking for the bathroom. I stayed there, very still thinking he would go away, but I kept one eye open, pretending I was asleep. He just stood at my door and stared at me. His unwelcomed presence at my opened door made me feel very uncomfortable! My bedroom sanctuary was now invaded and I had no idea what he would do next! He stood at my door watching me for what seemed like an eternity. Eventually he left, closing my bedroom door behind him. The very next day I bought and installed a lock for my door.

That is when my ordinary and independent life took an unexpected turn....

Fridays meant more customers due to the approaching weekend, so customer lines were longer, plus the extra waiting sometimes made customers grumpy. Those grumpy customers often grouched at the tellers which sometimes caused us to make mistakes. Smaller transaction amounts needed no authorization, but bank protocol demanded that any check cashed for money over six hundred dollars would need approval from Mrs. Mason, my supervisor. My next customers in the extremely long line were two cowboys all 'duded' up in their cowboy Sunday attire. The first thought that struck me was that they came from a western show. Perched on their heads were white, felt, Stetson, cowboy hats, thick, colorful, cotton shirts festooned with rhinestones and fringe on the sleeves, plus fancy cowboy boots. The cowboy with dark hair tipped his hat and said, "Howdy Ma'am, I would like to cash this check." After looking at the amount of the check, I knew I had to get Mrs. Mason's approval. I excused myself and went over to Mrs. Mason's desk. She looked at the check, and then glanced up at my customers. After she had recovered from the initial surprise of seeing cowboys in "her" bank, then recognized one of them, she approved the amount of the check and asked me to get two autographs for her two small boys. She told me the dark-haired cowboy was Montie Montana, Jr., a famous performer and showman. When I return to my teller window, I counted out the cash to him, asking him for three autographs (one for me and two for Mrs. Mason's sons). Montie signed his name quickly to the two autographs for Mrs. Mason's boys, but took a little longer on the last one, writing a bit longer. When he had finished, he folded that one sheet, then passed me all three of the autographs, motioning the folded one was mine. In my professional setting, all I could say was, "Thank you," and stored the note away until the long line of customers dwindled.

It wasn't until my lunch break that I had an opportunity to open the signed note to me. It read, "Howdy, Ma'am. I'm really impressed with your smile and personality. How would you like to join a Wild West Show? I will contact you in a week or two and we will discuss this more. Montie Montana, Jr." For some reason, I caught his eye. I was so surprised and a little skeptical about the wording of the note. Was he really interested in me for his show or just wanted to "try to trap me" into a date?

I showed the few employees in the lunchroom my note, which stated in part that he would call me in a week or so. Some of them laughed, since they thought what he wrote were half-truths to try to get a date from a pretty faced gal like me. I decided to laugh with them, dismissing the contents of the note as a prank, and went back to work. In the back of my mind, though, I really wondered if this cowboy was telling the truth. I would just have to wait and see....

Chapter 2

Anticipation of Adventure

Ever since the cowboy came into the bank, I caught myself fantasizing that he would indeed call. I was so eager for an adventurous change in my life! I wanted to travel so much!! The bank employees made comments to me more than once about my pretty face and figure, firmly believing every guy that looked at me either thought about asking for a date. What exactly did this cowboy want, a date or an employee? This nagging question was beginning to really bother and annoy me. I just had to know the answer!

On Monday morning at eight am, the bank had its usual staff meeting before it opened for business at nine. The Vice-President of the bank gave awards to several employees in different categories for a job well done. After fresh donuts and coffee, we prepared to open the bank. I set up my cash drawer, opened my teller window and waited for the front door to be unlocked and opened. About mid-morning the phone rang at my supervisor's desk. For some peculiar reason the sound of the phone ringing captured my attention. As I watched out of the corner of my eye, Mrs. Mason answered the ringing phone at her desk. I realized by her reaction that this wasn't an ordinary customer's call. I saw Mrs. Mason glance up at me, and then made a beeline to my teller's station. "You have a call," she said. I finished with my customer, put a closed sign at my teller window, and walked over to the phone....a call that would change my life forever.

The conversation went something like this: "Howdy, Chyrle! This is Montie Montana, Jr. How are you? Do you have time to meet a few of us at the restaurant by the Orange County Airport around six pm today? Our plane gets in around five-thirty pm."
"Sure," I said.
"We will see you then."

My hand was shaking as I hung up the phone and it was all I could do not to shout to everyone in the bank what I had just agreed to do for the evening! I still wasn't exactly sure what this meeting was all about, but I was none-the-less excited! As calmly as I could, I walked back to my station. I tried to focus on the customers who lined up to my now open window.

The rest of the day at the bank seemed to crawl by until the doors finally closed! After finishing the after-closing tasks for the day, I just had enough time to fix my hair and freshen up my make-up before I drove to the restaurant. I sure wasn't going to meet these gentlemen without a first-class touch-up!

As I climbed into my orange Volkswagen, I became very jittery. I had a difficult time focusing on where I was going and even how to drive! When I arrived, I somehow managed to find a parking spot and walked quickly to the front door. I was pretty sure I was the first to arrive since after a brief survey of the restaurant I didn't see anyone in cowboy garb, so I sat in the lobby and waited. After a few minutes of nervous waiting, in they strode, loaded with large cowboy hats, boots and several briefcases. I stood up and felt my nerves jump even more. Montie Montana, Jr., said, "Howdy, Ma'am. It's good to see you again! Let's go to the back conference room of the restaurant." I nervously smiled as I followed them.

We walked into the conference room where there was a large table and several chairs. Montie Montana, Jr. began to tell me the story of the Buffalo Bill's Wild West Show and Congress of Rough Riders of the World.

It was a re-creation of the original show, he explained. He had brought a bundle of pictures of the performers for me to see. I was really impressed! He said that when he talked to me that day in the bank and saw my smile plus my personality, he thought I would be perfect as the Public Relation Spokesperson who would go ahead of the performers, promoting the show. "I have no experience in doing public relation work," I objected! "I can't even ride a horse."

All you need to do is be yourself and we'll teach you the rest. Are you interested?" asked Montie.

"YES!" I exclaimed. I couldn't say it fast enough. My heart was racing with exhilaration. "What do I do next?" I asked.

"We need to get you outfitted with several western costumes and get you a passport. The next show will be ready to go on the road in two months." I realized, as my mind raced, this would mean that I would have to give a proper two-week notice of quitting my job at the bank. This notice allowed the bank to hire and train someone to take my place upon my departure. I almost missed his next question. "Can you store your car and personal things at your parents place or in storage?" asked Montie.

"Sure," I agreed, "That's not a problem."

"There's this small show we are doing back in Montana that we will be doing next week. It will run for 5 days, and then we will return to get you outfitted for the tour." Montie gave me his phone number in case I had any questions and handed me several bills to pay for my passport. Just before we all left, he turned to me and said, "Welcome aboard! It will be great to have you with us."

When I arrived at work the next day, I went about my usual routine of placing my personal items in my locker, putting my lunch in the break room refrigerator, picking up my cash drawer from the vault and chatting with different co-workers as they also went about their morning routine, preparing for the bank to open. But inside I was ready to burst! As I passed Mrs. Mason's desk on my way to my window, she eagerly asked how last evening had gone. I thought I was going to burst with excitement as I shared my experience! She was thrilled for me! She gushed, "It's a chance in a lifetime and something tells me you will be very successful! So now, you need to give us your two weeks' notice, right?"

"Yes," I affirmed. That day, word traveled around to the other employees and I was probably the most well regarded person working there!

My notion was to go home that afternoon and talk to my roommate about the upcoming changes in my future. One thing I will say, things had a way of working out. As I talked to her later, Judy knew someone who was looking for a place to live. Coincidentally, our apartment would work out great for this friend, plus I would not be leaving Judy without a roommate. Wednesday arrived with me not feeling like working since my mind was definitely distracted, but I needed the paycheck, so I half-heartedly went to work. After work, I called my parents to share the exciting news. I don't think my dad was too thrilled with the idea of me joining a Wild West Show. He didn't see how traveling here and there should take the place of a full education, since it was his plan I would complete college, then find a secure, steady career. He wanted so much for me to go beyond a high school education. My mom, on the other hand, was very supportive. I asked if I could store my car and clothes at their place. My mom readily agreed, with my father reluctantly supporting the idea. So now I just needed to figure out a way to get all my stuff to their house.

Relief! All my list of "to-dos" was being accomplished, but I panicked, when I thought of how soon I would hear from Montie Montana.

Friday, I was caught off-guard when Montie Montana called me at the bank – I thought I had allowed enough time for a full two-week notice! Relief flooded my soul when he explained he only needed me to meet him at a top western designer shop named "Newdies" in Los Angeles on Saturday afternoon around two pm for costume fittings. "Sure," I said. "I'll be there!"

Chapter 3

This is How It's Done, Ma'am

Saturday, as I drove to downtown Los Angeles, I got lost thanks to traffic and confusing overhead freeway signs. I turned off at the next exit and pulled into a gas station where the attendant told me I needed to return to the freeway and get off two exits further down. Even though this mistake took much longer than I had planned for the trip, miraculously I still made it on time! Montie is a very punctual person and I wanted him to think well of me.

I parked the car and stood in front of this small, unassuming western shop with Montie. I had never been fitted for a costume before, so I was a bit apprehensive about this new experience. As we entered the shop, I was introduced to Newdie. He reminded me of a Hollywood clothing designer in both mannerisms and the way he dressed. What an outfit he had on! From the hat perched comfortably on top of his head to the beautifully designed leather boots, Newdie was all class! His hair under his hat was dark, but what really stood out to me were his eyeglasses. The heavy black-rimmed eyewear didn't exactly strike me as western. Newdie acknowledged my presence with a nod, and then he began discussing with Montie the reason for our visit. As Montie described the look he wanted for my costumes, my eyes began to travel around the small shop. Newdie didn't have many items out, since he custom-made all of his costumes, but what was displayed was breathtaking and beautiful. Exquisite colorful designs using abundant amounts of rhinestones embellished the garments. Every conceivable design was present! Stars and flowers were most prevalently used, but other designs included butterflies, zigzagged lines, and guitars. Elvis Presley was one of his customers, so Newdie's designs reflected "The King's" presence considerably. I casually glanced at a price tag, and almost gasped aloud. The cost of one complete outfit was extremely expensive! How could I afford such luxury?! Then I remembered Montie telling me he would be covering the cost. I quietly heaved a sigh in relief.

I overheard Montie describe to Newdie that one costume was to be made out of leather (vest and skirt) and the other costume was to have two pairs of rhinestone pants (one jacket, two pairs of pants). Newdie then turned to me and asked, "What design would you like on your rhinestone jacket?" Since I love butterflies, I choose that as the design. Both outfits would be made and ready to pick up in two weeks. When the costumes were later delivered, the jacket was graced with colorful rhinestone butterflies on the front and a large one on the back.

After Newdie measured me for the outfits and we left the shop, Montie asked me if I would like to follow him in my car to his dad's ranch nearby. When I arrived, I saw some cowboys playing with ropes, their saddled horses tied to the nearby corral. Getting out of the car, I could smell food cooking on a barbeque around the corner of the barn, just out of sight. Montie Jr. introduced me to his dad, Montie Montana, Sr., and the rest of his cowboy friends who had just walked up to the cars to greet us. These guys sure looked like experts at roping and riding!

One of the cowboys in the group moved back to where he was originally standing and called me to join him. He handed me a coiled rope. "See that fake steer head on the fence? See if you can rope it," he directed. He then demonstrated what he wanted, and handed me the rope. This looks like fun! But it was really hard to stare straight ahead at the steer head and swing a rope at the same time. Plus the cowboy was right-handed where I am left-handed. All eyes turned to what I was about to do. Was I to swing the rope clockwise or counter clockwise? I just didn't know! I managed to keep the loop open, but when I let go, the loop flew behind me and looped a cowboy lookin' on.

Laughter came from the cowboys watching. I had to admit, the scene did look pretty funny. The cowboy that was lassoed laughed so hard, that he almost fell down! Then they urged, "Let's get her on a horse."
"But I don't ride," I objected strongly. I looked over at Montie for help and could tell he was eager to say something.
"Hold on guys, give the girl a break!" he drawled. But I just knew I was going to end up on a horse!

Montie said to me, "There's a lot to learn before you get on this horse."
I noticed a beautiful palomino horse, with a diamond on his forehead, tied to the fence a few yards down the corral fence. Montie instructed, "You start by firmly taking his reins in your hands, then lead the horse forward and then backing him up. Then you walk the horse around in one circular direction, and then go the other direction. This lets the horse know you are in charge. You mount the horse only from the left side, putting your left foot in the stirrup of the saddle and, swinging your right leg over -you're on. Let's see how you do."

I figured (as the cowboys say) "if it's going to be, it was up to me"! (which means this was something I needed to do by myself) I was "shaking in my boots" (cowboy slang) even though I was literally wearing white tennis shoes! I let the horse know exactly what I was about to do. I will say my long legs helped me mount the horse. But after I got on the horse, it didn't move. I was stuck wondering how to get this horse to budge.

15

My right hand was tightly clutching the saddle horn while my left hand held the reins. Since the horse was fairly tall (about fifteen to sixteen hands, where each hand equals about five inches), I felt like I was far off the ground. This made me feel like I could fall off! How could I keep in the saddle while prompting this horse to move?! Somehow I did manage to get the palomino to move forward a couple of steps. Much to my dismay, one of the cowboys smacked the horse on the rump which caused the horse to bolt and buck! I tried to hold on, but ended up flipping through the air and landing flat on my rear.

The cowboys figured the horse would run, not buck, but they laughed at how I landed. Montie quickly moved to help me up and brought me over to the barbeque pit area to rest and recover from my fall. He was furious at those guys! I was shaken and sore, but at least I could move and gingerly sat down. Fortunately, nothing seemed broken. The cowboy felt so ashamed that he came over to me and gave me his rope. "Here, you earned it," he said apologetically.

As I sat at the picnic table trying to catch my breath, Montie, Jr. returned with a soda for me. After Montie, Jr. left and I began to sip the soda that I realized that there were bowls of food sending out wonderful aromas in the center of the table, and Montie, Sr.'s wife was bringing out even more food! Turning my head I saw a couple of cowboy cooks at the barbeque pit cooking steaks. Everyone began gathering around the table where I was sitting, picking up plates, and lining up for their "grub". Montie, Jr. returned to invite me to join the line for the food. After claiming a large steak and a small scoop of chili beans at the barbeque spit, I limped back to the picnic table that was furnished with bowls of potato salad, coleslaw, and a plate heaping with garlic bread.

After the delicious barbeque, the cowboys got out their guitars and sang a few contemporary and western songs.

After my experience that afternoon with the horse and rope, I began to seriously doubt that I was cut out for this kind of life style.

I was extremely thankful that I didn't have work the next day since it was Sunday. I felt very sore after being bucked off the horse!

Monday I woke up filled with excitement! This was going to be my last week as a teller. A new girl had been hired to take over my position. Now it was my turn to train her for the job. My replacement was nervous! I remembered how nervous I was and how hard I had tried my first days at the job. I encouraged her and reassured her that she was doing a first- rate job. By the end of the day, I felt convinced that she was going to be a good teller.

Wednesday the bank closed at five pm. My drawer balanced and I managed to get over to the passport office before it closed at six. My picture was taken and I paid for the passport with the money Montie had given me. I was told by the clerk that I would have to wait two weeks before receiving the passport in the mail.

On Friday as I gathered up my jacket and lunch box for the final time, I said my good-byes to Mrs. Mason and all the bank staff. Everyone wished me well. As I walked to my car, I felt a bit apprehensive about this change in my life. In fact, my new job description was still very vague to me. All I knew was that now I had committed to becoming a Public Relations Person for a western show. I could not help but be unsure about the new adventure in my life and was left with an

uncomfortable feeling of reluctance and yet excitement, too. I anticipated the unexpected and moved forward with just a little bit of fear.

On Saturday, I received a call from Montie. He had been very busy at the Navajo Indian Reservation auditioning for the traveling show. The Navajo Hoop Dance and the Navajo War Dance were just a few of the Navajo ceremonies he wanted for the show.

I was counting the days with enthusiasm to when the show was going to hit the road! Keeping busy boxing up all my clothes and belongings at the apartment and moving everything to my parents' garage over the next two weeks was what helped me to curb my impatience for the day of our departure.

Two weeks later found that I had everything in place! My belongings were moved to my parents' house, I received my passport, and I picked up my NEW western outfits. I was more than ready to go!

Just a few days before we left, Montie contacted me, expressing that he wanted me to learn something about the performers traveling in this touring show. Montie provided me with a book to read about the background of this amazing show. From the book I learned how Colonel William Frederick Cody, known as "Buffalo Bill", organized and presented a traveling exhibition in the late 1800's. This show consisted of Native American Indians performing different ceremonies. Also included were trick ropers, wagon train attacks, stage coach hold-ups, hide races (riders on cow-hides), an Australian whip cracker and a boomerang artist. Added to all this were bucking horses, trained horses that performed tricks on command, quick pistol-draw demonstrations, trick riders, Roman Riders, cancan dancers, stuntmen, buffalo, longhorn steers, mules, oxen and so much more.

Montie had re-created this traveling entertainment and was now going to take it not just through Europe, but all around the globe!

The background music was a prerecorded tape of fully orchestrated instrumental music ranging from western to patriotic to contemporary music – each piece fitting with the type of act performing. At the conclusion of every performance there was a gigantic fireworks display. For this upcoming show, Montie had assembled seventy-five top performers from around the world. It was going to be an extraordinary touring pageant!

Chapter 4

Departure... At Last!

Six am found me traveling to the Los Angeles International Airport. As soon as I arrived, Montie and five of his closest performer/friends, who were dressed in comfortable clothes for traveling, met me at the pre-arranged meeting spot in front of the airline terminal door. We went up to the airline counter where we all showed our passports and checked in our luggage. I was all fired up for this trip, but...where were we going?! In all the time-consuming arrangements proceeding this moment, I hadn't had the time to ask and Montie had not volunteered the information! Right before the flight Montie rounded us up telling us we were going; to Kuala Lumpur, Malaysia, with the possibility of more destinations to come. I managed to stay calm, but inside, I was jumping for joy and excitement!

We boarded the plane and I sat in the row with Montie, his secretary, Mary, and Jim, a photographer. In the row right behind us were Montie's son and daughter, Jess (fourteen years old) and Kelly (sixteen years old) plus three trick riders, Susan, Linda, and Debbie.

The three trick riders needed to find horses for the show beforehand. They left their own horses behind to eliminate the regulated two weeklong quarantine wait in Malaysia.

This plane was a Boeing 747 'Jumbo Jet', which was the largest jet to fly internationally. Even though it was huge from the outside, the seating arrangement was jammed. We rode in coach class, not in first class. First class had fewer seats with lots more legroom, but the cost was so much more, and with such a large group, Montie couldn't afford the price of those tickets! My pre-arranged middle seat didn't give me much legroom since I am very long- legged. Plus I had never traveled on a plane for over five hours and this was going to be a twenty-four hour flight. I wasn't sure how I was going to sleep sitting up. I finally succeeded to settle in by leaning my seat as far back as it would allow. I obtained a blanket from the flight attendant. Before I knew it, I had slept eight hours straight, missing two meals. Boy was I hungry! The next meal service, I ate everything.

I noticed that the two trick riders were barely polite to me, but as the flight continued they became almost hostile! I couldn't figure out what I had done wrong that caused them to treat me so badly, but during the flight, I overheard a whispered conversation that explained most of it. Two of the trick riders were asking in whispered tones to the other closely seated performers, why I was sitting up with Montie and the "leaders" but they were not! They reasoned THEY had been with Montie far longer than I, a "newbie". They had also heard how I knew nothing about roping or riding a horse, so I was NOT a "cowgirl". With these 'facts' firmly planted in their minds, they felt I was very much "beneath" them. They viewed me as an interloper, a no-body who cut into their right to have a possibly better job! My work was sure cut out for me being the PR spokesperson for these two - plus the rest of the troupe! I knew I would have to try really hard to be nice to them, so they would not be quite so jealous of me!

After twenty-four cramped hours of jet travel, we arrived in Kuala Lumpur, the federal capital of Malaysia. On a calendar we had actually flown two days instead of one, because we had crossed the International Date Line. We needed to exit the plane in full costume, as the TV press and reporters were to meet us after we went through customs. Montie, Debbie, Susan and I took turns dressing, brushing teeth and combing hair in the plane's small bathroom. Before landing we wanted to look as good as we could after being jammed into small seats for so long. I chose to put on my beautiful butterfly rhinestone pant suit, as I wanted to make a good impression and this was my favorite costume!

Once through customs with our luggage, we were pleasantly greeted by the reporters, press and our sponsor, Raszak from Mars Film, the company sponsoring us as we traveled through Malaysia. Raszak, like any Malaysian man, was dark olive-complexioned, short in stature and slight in build. Montie did some rope tricks for the press, while I just stood there holding a rope, looking on hoping I looked like I belonged with the troupe! I felt so out of place, so disconnected with this group of talented people. Raszak had two vans ready to take us to the hotel. I just couldn't believe how humid the weather was! Just after a few minutes outside, my clothes were sticking to me. The driver of the van had

to negotiate all sorts of traffic taking us through the middle of town to our hotel, located on the opposite side of the city from the airport. And the traffic! People were in cars, trucks, scooters, bicycles, and on foot. They were in front, beside, or behind the van - all moving in every conceivable direction! In this country, folks would walk or ride their bicycles or scooters on either side of the road, depending where they wanted to go and how they wanted to get to their destination! The motor vehicles were the only transportation that had a specific way to travel on these roads. The roads were either paved or dirt, depending on whether it was a main road or one on the outskirts of the town. Buildings were made primarily of concrete with grey as the prevalent color. The landscape turned dramatically from few trees to heavily-forested as we drove out of town. The vans had no air conditioning, plus the seating was jammed to capacity with people and luggage, so the ride was less than pleasant. When we arrived at the hotel, Montie told us we had the next two days off to catch up on our sleep.
Yeah! Glorious sleep!

After an enjoyable couple of days off, it was time for all of us to go to work. The two trick riders set out to find horses and livestock for the show. Using "new" horses for the riders was a huge hardship, since horse and rider were a "team" in every sense of the word! Trick riders depended on knowing their mount, down to how the horse was feeling on the day of the "stunt". Every step, every movement was anticipated by the horse and rider. If they made a wrong movement or step, it could mean death to the rider, the horse, or both. Other livestock needed included draft horses or oxen to pull wagons and steers for roping.

The rest of us climbed into the van with Raszak to inspect the sports arena which was just a few minutes from our hotel at the edge of town. From afar the arena looked small, but as we drew near to the site it was actually BIG inside and out! The seating capacity of this building was approximately ten thousand around a huge arena. The seats graduated up at an angle, so the audience had a clear view of whatever entertainment was being performed below.

I saw firsthand all the work required to make a show come to life. Included were all the behind-the-scenes day-to-day problems that had to be resolved before opening day. In this case, truckload after truckload of dirt had to be transported into the facility to fill the arena floor for the best footing for the animals. A western town prop had to be built, so truckloads of wood, paint, and equipment for building the set were transported from different locations within the city. As for the language barrier, Montie had no trouble speaking and understanding Malaysian, since he seemed to be able to "pick up" different languages quickly. As for me, I had only learned to say "thank you" in Malaysian, which is "Terima Kasia."

Our group interpreter showed up that afternoon. I would have two weeks to learn as much of the language as I could! I sure hoped this interpreter had a lot of patience!

Meanwhile, the trick riders found the only horses that were available in the city area, but they were polo horses. Polo horses were trained to lean from side to side, so the polo rider would be able to hit the ball to the goal line. The trick riders needed horses to run level, so they would be able stand on the backs of the horses to do the different stunts required. Our girls knew they had their job cut out for them, since they would have to work with these horses every day for hours attempting to retrain them to trot for stunt work.

After the first language lesson, I needed to get serious and learn enough Malaysian for the speech I would have to give at the end of the show, so I invited Sherry, the interpreter, to come up to my room. I kept practicing the few sentences I needed for this speech, writing and saying them repeatedly to get them memorized.
Since we landed in Malaysia, the trick riders had been gossiping to the Roman Riders and now both groups were being cold to me! I didn't realize how jealous they all were until I overheard another conversation they were all having about me! I "couldn't ride a horse". I had "no experience in the Western show field". I "couldn't work a rope very well". On and on the petty comments flew until I made some movement noise letting them know I was coming. Boy did they all stop talking and even looked a bit sheepish! I hadn't realized

how rough and tough these gals were and how quick they were to judge me! I just didn't know how I would ever win them over!

To tell you the truth, the gossip really depressed me. I started to feel I was rather useless, since I didn't know anything about roping or riding a horse, plus the language was extremely difficult to learn.

I began to feel very unsure about the whole venture. Perhaps I shouldn't be paid for what I "couldn't do". I approached Montie to see if he could show me a rope trick. Maybe, at least, I could do THAT! He checked his calendar, finding he had some time after lunch to work with me. I was so excited, believing it would be no time before I would be spinning a rope. WRONG! Trust me, it's hard! There are no wires or "tricks" in this type of rope! Add to that, I am left-handed and Montie is right. He opened the loop of the rope up for me using his right hand and spun a flat loop. Then I took it with my right hand and tried to keep it going. It felt strange using my right hand, but I keep the loop going for three turns before it stopped spinning. Now it was my turn to open the loop on my own. Timing is everything in opening that loop up! I would throw it out to begin the loop, but it didn't work. I tried again, but it still didn't work. I tried over and over again, without any success. Sure looked like I had better practice a lot if I was to ever learn to rope! A letter arrived from home on Wednesday. Uh, oh! Bad news? Nope, just a newsy letter from my mom. I was excited to hear from home, plus holding the letter reminded me I was a bit homesick too! Before I left I had lamented to my mom how I couldn't ride a horse, couldn't rope, and, as far as I knew, I had no ancestors that were "cowboys"! How was I going to be able to fit into this western group?! I didn't feel like a 'cowgirl' at all! She related in her letter that she had done some investigating into our family ancestors and had found out that our heritage was traced back to a Cherokee tribe! My great-grandmother, Princess Rose, was honored by Will Rogers's father in the first school of Native Americans set up by the United States Government.

I was one-eighth Cherokee! Also, she had chatted with my Aunt Jo Gates, who related to her that she was once engaged to the grandson of Buffalo Bill Cody, but changed her mind and didn't marry him. If she had, I would have had some of the Cody blood running through my veins as well! I was actually very relieved to get this letter and showed Montie. I had heard some of the performers questioning Montie as to why he had chosen me to represent the show when I had no western background or talent. Now I could stand up tall and say, "Yes, I do!" Thanks, Mom! Perhaps fate had a hand in my meeting with Montie that day at the bank teller window. I will probably never know...

Today I spent half of the day cramming to learn the Malaysian language and the other half practicing my roping. I really wanted to figure out how to do the flat loop with the rope so I could perform it well in the arena. I couldn't get any of the troupe members to work with me, so I had to tackle it by myself. I tried my best to spin the rope with my right hand the way Montie taught me, but every time the rope would snarl up, drag on the floor or hit my body and stop. I was getting so frustrated! I would throw the rope down, but something drove me to keep picking it up again. Would I ever get this rope trick right?!! My right arm and wrist became so sore I decided to take the rope in my left hand to spin it. With the very first attempt, the rope spun into a flat loop for about two rotations. Wow! This is working!! Maybe I could be a "cowgirl" after all!

Chapter 5

My First Show

Montie had everyone meet together after breakfast. During one of the meetings with Montie, Raszak, and the hotel management, someone from the hotel management group suggested our troupe perform a sampling of our show as a 'warm up' before the main act that had already been engaged. This would be good for our troupe to perform to a crowd whose culture had no frame of reference to what a "cowboy" or an "Indian" was and might possibly boost ticket sales. The hotel would benefit, since they booked different acts in their lounge on Saturday nights, which could hold a paying audience of up to about six hundred. Of course the trick rides couldn't be on the stage, since they needed their horses and an arena to perform their stunts. The program would consist of Montie, who could rope and sing Cowboy songs, the whip artist from Australia, and....me. WHAT!! I had to go on stage and perform! I didn't know the first thing about performing! And the only thing I could do was a flat loop - barely!

We were to meet in the stage dressing room by seven pm. I was dressed in my rhinestone butterfly outfit, clutching my rope, sick to my stomach with terror! Montie told each of us as we arrived where we were on the performance schedule. As I walked through the door, Montie caught a look at my face - drained of color from fear. My eyes began to tear up as I struggled to move by him. I didn't want to do this AT ALL!

"What's wrong?" he asked softly.

"I can't do this!" I whispered to him. He immediately grabbed my arm, lead me into another room and sat me down. Montie knew from experience what was going on in my head. Stage fright had hit me big time!! He confided, "The secret is not to look at the audience, but think of yourself spinning your rope by yourself in your room."

I did my best to visualize what he said, but it just wasn't working. Montie realized that his suggestion was ineffective and then asked if I had ever been hypnotized. "No," I said. He gently shoved me deeper into the softly cushioned chair, telling me to relax and breathe deeply. He began to count down from ten. As I focused on his voice, I felt as if I was being soothed in a warm bathtub, relaxed and sleepy. I don't remember what he said to me after that or how much time had elapsed, but when I opened my eyes, I felt very calm. Montie observed my calmness and confidently stated, "Let's go." So we both left the room, rejoining the others who were waiting for our act to begin.

When my turn finally came, Montie, who was now stationed on stage to introduce each part of our show, introduced me and called me to join him. I confidently stepped out, smiling towards the audience. I knew this was a "full house", since the lounge could seat six hundred people, but this knowledge did not bother me. Remarkably I wasn't frightened at all! The spotlights shone on me and all I could see was darkness out where the audience was sitting. At this point, I realized that I could be anywhere practicing my routine, rather than in front of this audience. With the rope in my left hand, I started spinning. It only took me about two seconds of spinning the flat loop to decide to jump into the center of the rope which I had not attempted in any of my practice sessions. I jumped in, then jumped out, took a lady's bow and left the stage. I did it, I did it, I DID it!!

After the show, Montie walked by me whispering conspiratorially, "Great job!"

The next few days were going to be very busy for Montie as the remainder of the show performers showed up. We now had exactly one week before OPENING DAY. I had an interview scheduled with the local television news station that reached a huge audience. I also had an interview with the main city newspaper and one of its photographers.

After a week of intense language practicing with my interpreter, I felt much more prepared for the television interviews that were scheduled for the day. Montie, the interpreter, and I met in the lobby of the hotel to drive over to the TV station in a white Mars Film Production van. We were dropped off at the front door, walked inside, then upstairs, where we were greeted by a man on of the television stage set. We had five minutes until we went on the air. It was live TV!

Montie walked out on the set first. He had his guitar on a strap slung over his shoulder. Then I followed clutching a rope, with the interpreter following me. Montie had so much confidence! He chatted so easily with the interviewer! When it was my turn to talk, I conveyed the dates of the Buffalo Bill's Wild West Show including the show times, plus gave a brief description of what acts would be in the show. I gave the whole speech in Malaysian. After my brief and rather shaky interview, Montie sang a cowboy song after which I spun a flat loop. That was it . . . we were done. It was my very first appearance on television! I felt so excited and a bit proud of my performance! That evening we tuned in the news at six o'clock. Halfway into the program, our interview came on. How fun it was to see us on television! The cameraman did several close ups of my western butterfly outfit with me spinning the rope. I wondered if the trick riders were a little jealous, because they were rather quiet after the news went off the air.

That morning at ten am I had an appointment with a local newspaper and needed to be in full western costume. This time I wore the leather outfit and grabbed my rope. The reporters, photographer, my interpreter, and I went to the sports arena in Raszak's van where I saw Montie in the sound booth that was positioned way up over the arena where he was working on the music and sound for the show. I hadn't been to the arena in days and, wow, had it changed! The whole arena was filled in with dirt and the western Frontier Town was completed. The news reporter chose to do the photo shoot in front of the Frontier Town. The trick riders were practicing on horseback on the outskirts of the arena, stirring up a lot of dust during the entire interview.

I posed for photos in front of the dance hall, then in front of the saloon and the hitching post. It helped that I had done some modeling in the past to know how to pose. After the pictures, and with the aid of Sherry our interpreter, I answered questions asked by the reporter. I felt uneasy with the trick riders watching my interview as they practiced on horseback. I'm sure they gave me dirty looks as they rode around in the arena. I figured the girls would say something to Montie later about all the attention I was getting. But lucky for me, the photographer wanted a few pictures of them practicing on their horses. Maybe that will ease some of the jealousy and complaining I thought.

More performers were to arrive at the airport Thursday around seven pm with Raszak arranging to pick up the group in a large touring bus. The first chance I had to meet everyone was the next morning at breakfast. I spent a good amount of time introducing myself to the group, and then later worked on trying to remember the new arrivals' names. To be a good Public Relation spokesperson I needed to know something about each performer, plus his or her talent. On the short and humid bus ride to the sports arena, I observed the actors who were in the show. 'Buffalo Bill Cody' was played by Rudy Robbins, who actually shared some physical characteristics of Buffalo Bill. There were about ten Native Americans for the different Native American dances and the wagon train attack. John Brady was the Australian boomerang thrower and whip artist. Also aboard were twenty cowboys and cowgirls who performed different acts in the show, such as Cancan dancing, doing dangerous stunts in the western gunfight and wagon train attack, and portraying civil war soldiers. I sat in the bus wondering how a girl like me could be so lucky as to experience all of this!

Everyone who had to ride horses in the show now had to have the additional burden of dealing with untrained steeds. Especially affected were the trick riders, Roman Riders, and those who drove the teams of horses in both the wagon train chase and stagecoach run. These horses were trained to chase a little white ball, anticipating the rider's movements who were leaning to hit the ball with a mallet. So these poor, confused animals now had to deal with NOT leaning from side to side, but run straight and steady! Equally, the riders were used to their own personal mounts, to the point that they could anticipate, feel, and time the gait of their individual horses. To say the least, these riders and horses were going to have a difficult time just becoming familiar with each other, in such a short amount of time. So a lot of practice was really important for the safety of both horse and rider!

On Saturday, every performer was as ready as they could be for our first Malaysian show. The bleachers were filled to capacity. Buffalo Bill rode into the center arena astride a beautifully groomed, proud, white horse. The horse pulled a front leg back, lowered his head down in a bow and Buffalo Bill announced, "Let the show begin!" The stagecoach came rolling in with six horses in full stride, thrilling the audience as it circled around the arena twice before exiting. Montie, up in the announcer's booth, broadcasted the show in English while a Malaysian broadcaster translated it to the crowd. The audience roared with excitement as the show continued with trick riders, Roman Riders, stage coach hold ups, stunt men, saloon Cancan dancers and Native American hoop dance. What an action-packed show! I was jumping for joy hearing the crowd behind the stage as one act following another moved out into the arena. I was extremely excited to be part of this great show!

I couldn't help but notice the Australian performers, John and Vi Brady. After watching this couples' act, I had no doubt in my mind what I wanted to do - become a trick rope artist. After the show, I hurried onto the bus to sit next to them, just to be close to them. Vi and John were about fifteen years older than me. They both had incredible elegance on and off stage, not at all the rough-and-tumble, tobacco chewing ruffians and trouble-makers of the typical Wild West group. These two had an aura about them of warmth, friendliness, and true graciousness. This attitude drew me to aspire to be just like Vi Brady one day. In the show, she flicked a white shirt button from John's tongue with a ten foot bull whip at first strike.

John Brady

WOW! And John was probably the most talented cowboy I had ever seen. He could do incredibly difficult rope tricks. When he was at the end of a rope, it could almost dance! He was the best in the world in doing rope routines ever done on foot or on horseback. He did whip cracking with Australian bull and stock whips plus threw different size boomerangs out over the audience's heads, upwards to twenty-five feet away. Unbelievable!

On Wednesday there were two duplicate shows, one at one pm and the other at five pm. After a buffet breakfast, I went back to my room to get the things I needed to take to the arena. As I was about to depart, I noticed the message light on my phone blinking. I picked up the earpiece, dialed for voicemail, and listened to the message which stated, "My name is Prince Andrew. I saw you on television last week and saw you in the local magazine. I would very much like to meet you. Please call me." I immediately called Montie, telling him about the message. Because this man was a prince, I was overwhelmed and uncertain how to respond. Montie thought it was pretty cool. "Call him back to arrange to meet him at the hotel and I will be there to check him out." I called back the phone number the prince had left at the end of the message and his social secretary answered. He arranged a meeting with the prince and I in the hotel lobby around eight pm that night.

After the final show of the day, I changed into a dinner dress and headed down to the lobby of the hotel, where Montie was waiting for me. Just a few minutes later, a black limousine drove up to the front entrance. Two muscled, Malaysian bodyguards emerged from the limo with the prince immediately following. Both men were very aware of every person around the prince and were imposing! By the way they acted, I felt these two men would die to protect their leader! My focus then turned to the Prince. He was wearing a traditional man's Malaysian outfit with a very bright headpiece perched on his head. About my height, this man was very handsome! He was clean-shaven with dark, olive-complexioned skin, deep, brown eyes, and a captivating smile. He strode purposefully into the lobby, scanning the area for me. His course changed as he noted my location. As he approached, I did a little bow and I extended my right hand to shake his. The Prince gently took my hand, leaned over and respectfully kissed it. I was all smiles, but uncertain what to do next. Out of the corner of my eye I noticed Montie's movement, so I introduced him to the prince. After their greeting, we all proceeded into the hotel lounge with a bodyguard leading the way and one following us. Prince Andrew selected a private booth. He spoke limited English, which made it difficult to understand him, but still it was a much easier conversation than speaking strictly in Malaysian. He proclaimed to Montie that he wanted to court me and, if things worked out, take me as his wife. Montie immediately refused this offer, explaining that I was an employee of the Buffalo Bill's Wild West Show and, as an employee, had responsibilities and obligations to fulfill. Prince Andrew would not be put off so easily, however. He pursued his interests to possibly marry me by explaining his cultural background and how well cared for I would be. His explanation continued and, what finally caught my attention enough to stop being so dreamy over this man, was the Islamic Malaysian cultural accepted practice of polygamy. He further explained he had two wives already, wishing to take me for a third! Wow! That was a shock! Fast-talking Montie, continuing to disarm this awkward situation, re-explained to him that the prince's courting me would not work as I had signed a contract with the Show and thus could not be free to choose. At first Prince Andrew was furious, since he was very accustomed to always getting his desire, and especially since he considered it to be a gracious and generous offer. Finally, he had to relent, since Montie was adamant about me being under contract. He acknowledged Montie's decision affirming, "I will just wait until the contract is up." He then exited to his car with his bodyguards in front and behind him. My head was still spinning over the conversation as I left for my room. Prince Andrew continued to call me daily and to send flowers to my room. It wasn't until we left Kuala Lumpur that he lost contact with me, as we were constantly on the move.

I had previously mentioned to Montie that I did have other talents. I had been in a local beauty pageant while in high school. My talent in the pageant was Hawaiian dancing. After my chatting about my dancing, he told me about the many ranches on the big island of Hawaii and about the Paneola Cowboys. "Why wait! Let's get you in the show and call you a Paneola Cowgirl." Within a week, I had received a Hawaiian costume, which included a grass shirt, a bathing suit-type top, a headdress, a breath-taking beautiful floral lei, and two Uli Uli's, which are decorative, hand-held noise makers - all in the mail from Hawaii. I put the costume on and it fit perfectly.

Chyrle Bacon
"Paneola Cowgirl"

Chapter 6

A New Town

Montie was very pleased with the two week run in Kuala Lumpur. Now it was time to drive road to the small town of Kelantan, Malaysia. Kelantan was about a two hour drive by car, but with the traveling show including stage coaches, wagons, performers and props, the trip would be anything, but easy! The travel time took much longer. Along the way, we saw a few small rough-hewed, broken-down shacks selling crocodile-skin bags and wallets. After about an hour of hot, humid travel, everyone wanted to stop and cool off with a drink. Down the road a piece farther, we came upon a large area that included another run-down, open-market-style gift shop and on the side were enclosure pens with captured crocodiles. A sign stated "Crocodile Farm".

The buses pulled into a dirt area marked off somewhat for vehicular parking and we piled out for a potty break, a cool drink, and some possible shopping. I immediately began to tug on Montie's sleeve, proclaiming that I really didn't have to potty THAT much, this place was REALLY worn down, the fence enclosures around the crocodiles looked like they were ready to fall apart, and I DON'T like crocodiles! I didn't feel we were very protected if one of those ugly creatures wanted to get out!

After I visited the potty and purchased a somewhat cool drink, I wandered over to what looked like an empty pen. While waiting for the rest of the group, I decided to peek over the fenced enclosure. There was a crocodile far in the back! I leaned j-u-s-t a bit more, adding pressure to the already rickety wood fence to get a better look, when the fence gave way!

Now the fence was on its side with me IN the pen! Panic set in since I wasn't exactly sure of the crocodile's location within this mucky, muddy enclosure! I just leapt up and scrambled out as fast as I could! I was filthy, but so relieved! The staff at the farm quickly came to repair the fence when they heard my scream and saw what happened. As they were repairing the fence, I noticed that the crocodile had moved....closer to me and almost escaped! I also realized the some of the staff had sharp long sticks they were using to keep the croc back away from the ongoing repairs. WOW!! I had not realized this croc was so HUGE!! To add to my now icky misery, the whole group had heard the commotion and had wandered over to see what had happened! So, my backside was covered in stinky mud. I was humiliated and almost in tears, all because I was curious!

By now everyone had been somewhat refreshed, so we boarded the buses. It was bad enough that I had fallen into the crocodile pen, but to make the situation even more dramatic, I was muddy from the process, and my clothes reeked of mud and crocodile poop! I had used some wet paper towels from the restroom to clean up, but it didn't help very much. Some of the trick riders on the bus got a really good laugh over my clumsiness. And, you guessed it; NO one wanted to sit next to me, especially my muddy side!! I sure felt like being billed as the "Crocodile Lady"! And I am sure several on the bus were possibly thinking the same thing!! Since we made our unplanned stop and my accident added to further delay us, the caravan caught up to the buses. Farther and farther back into the jungle the winding, dirt road took us. The road seemed to continually grow narrower as we progressed along. Ahead was the first intersection that we had seen in about an hour. In the middle of the road were soldiers standing and watching us as we approached. I felt very uncomfortable which quickly turned to almost sheer terror! The men were armed Communist Guerillas with double breasted ammunition belts across their chests and machine guns pointed directly at US!

When we left the city, we knew we would be just a few miles from the Thailand border where the Communists were infiltrating the surrounding nearby area. We figured the locale we would be traveling through wasn't close enough to any Communist activity, so this was an extremely dangerous surprise! These soldiers would occasionally come across this portion of border, so we just happened to be at the wrong place at the wrong time. I actually believed we were all going to die! Montie told us to stay calm and not to look at them as we moved slowly through the crossing and continued down the road. Every one of us on the bus did exactly what we were told. God must have been with us that day because we got through just fine.

About two tiring and tense hours later, we knew we had arrived in the town of Kelantan for the road had somewhat widened. A few outbuildings announced their presence before we actually saw this hamlet. We all wanted to be free of the hot and stuffy buses, but before we could go to our motel we had to first help unload all the wagons and props at the arena from the vehicles that were following us. Also, we had brought along most of the animals needed for the show. They needed to be fed and watered after the long, slow journey. The sun had just set, but there was still enough light to view our new show location. The outdoor arena was not what I had expected, since the last sports arena was enclosed with air conditioning. This place had a definite rundown, unkempt appearance. Rough-hewn wood bleachers were available for the audience with a dirt arena and entrance. This arena had been "reclaimed" from the jungle, with no shade available to anyone, performers or audience. Well, at least no one had to haul in dirt! Wonderful, no air conditioning! We would all have to work in the heat and sweltering humidity!

At breakfast the next morning, Montie announced that a few of us were scheduled to visit a school, a crippled children's home and a hospital. I was included in these events and was super excited! It was fully rewarding to see those school children's faces as we performed in a small cafeteria at our first stop.

Dressed in our western garb, Vi and John Brady did some rope and whips, Montie played the guitar and sang, I did a little roping and the stuntmen did some really funny stunts which included falling down a lot. This event outline worked well for the next two locations we visited. The children laughed and applauded at all we did! It felt so wonderfully fulfilling to see children having such a good time! We knew those in the home and hospital wouldn't be able to come see the Wild West Show, so we did the best skits we could especially for them. This was absolutely the most rewarding day I had yet experienced.

After returning to the motel, we all changed our clothes, agreeing to meet at the restaurant adjacent to the property with the other show performers. While we were eating, Vi and John Brady asked Montie and the rest of the performers, "Why don't we give Chyrle the title 'Miss Wild West of the Buffalo Bill's Wild West Show'?" Montie was agreeable to the idea. "Well, Chyrle," Montie asked, "What do you think?"

YES, I ACCEPT! "Thank you, thank you, and thank you!" I kept saying. I became the first Miss Wild West of the present day Buffalo Bill's Wild West Show. A 'Miss Wild West' banner was made for me in town and I was to wear it everywhere.

I was so proud of my new title! After receiving the newly made banner, I stared in awe at it. Every time I took it off, I carefully laid it in a safe location, smoothing it out to keep it from wrinkling. Okay, maybe I didn't have to compete with other contestants for the title of Miss Wild West, but I did have to have the approval of the performers and that meant a lot to me! This gesture reassured me that I was an accepted part of the group!

The following day the trick riders spent a good deal of time looking for horses for the show. Since the location of the town was so secluded, not being close to any sports complexes, horses were difficult to find. Eventually, a retired racehorse farm was discovered. The owners were agreeable for us to use selected stock if Montie would sign a waiver agreeing that the horses would be returned to them in good condition and health, plus these owners would be not held accountable for any rider injuries. The trick riders were far from thrilled to have to use these horses, but no other choices were available. I just kept my fingers crossed that the horses would work for the trick riders as we only had two days for practice before the show opened.

This time I was on my own to do the special appearance with the newspaper reporters and TV station. Preparing a speech by myself was definitely a lot more difficult than I thought it would be. Montie was just too busy getting the arena ready. The day of the interview arrived. Even though I was enjoying all of the exclusive attention, there was an incessant gnawing deep down inside my gut that had me really worried. I just wanted everything to go well. I was ushered into a room where I saw a small crowd of people gathered around the TV cameras. I was introduced to the newscaster, prompted on where and when to give my speech, then we were on the air! My speech went great, but it took me three times to get the rope to spin before I could jump into it to do a trick called the "Cowboy Wedding Ring".

The interview seemed to extend forever, but in reality, lasted just a few moments and was suddenly over. OK, so maybe I could have done a better job, but I did the best I could by myself! I emerged from the room into the lobby to find a few people wanting my autograph. I was in my western outfit and a monitor was placed there for people to view whatever program was being shown at the moment. These folks who had just finished watching my interview thought I was someone really important! Since I have never ever signed an autograph before this day, I impulsively signed each one of their pieces of paper with a "BEST WISHES, MISS WILD WEST" message, quickly creating a logo that I still use today.

Being so excited and proud of myself, I didn't sleep too well that night thinking about my day of interviews and signing autographs. What an experience! And all by myself! But if I was now 'Miss Wild West', I had better learn more rope tricks!

On opening night the lights of the arena revealed a sold out audience including outdoor seating that was rather rickety. The female performers had their own small dressing room, as did the men. We rushed around this tiny area, trying to keep out of each other's way as we hurried to dress, all getting ready for multiple acts. This was to be my first performance as a Paneola Cowgirl. So I had three outfit changes to make, first going out in the stagecoach in my leather attire that included the banner of my new title, tearing back to change into my Hawaiian outfit, do my Paneola Cowgirl routine, then back to change into my other western outfit. Everything had to be set out just right, as this was my first time with so many costume changes! As the show was about to begin, I grabbed my rope, dashing out to the entrance of the arena. "Buffalo Bill Cody" came out to the center of the arena and said... "Let the show begin!" His white stallion bowed to the audience and he rode out of the arena.

The GRAND ENTRÉE! Usually, the cowboys and cowgirls on horseback were holding flags of different countries as they rode into the arena in single file, completing a full circle of the outside edge once. Then they would form a line facing one side of the audience for the Malaysian National Anthem. They turned to face the other side of the arena where the American National Anthem played. Finally, all horsemen would leave in single file circling the outside edge once again before exiting.

That night, however, we learned a very important lesson about those racehorses. If one got in front of the rest, even at a walk, the others would try to "catch and beat" the frontrunner!

...And that's exactly what happened! As the riders were reining the horses to walk in a single file, the horses trailing the leader sensed a race in progress and took off at full speed! FASTER, FASTER AND FASTER the horses carrying their riders ran around the arena as if it were a real horse race. The riders did all they could just to hold on! The Grand Entrée flags went flying off in all directions, landing everywhere and anywhere on the ground.

My position by the entrance of the gate allowed me to watch the people in the audience attempting to keep up with the horses and surprised riders. Montie announced to the gate- keepers to open the arena gate, allowing the horses and riders out. I clutched the side of the bleachers to keep out of the way of the out-of-control horses as they exited. Other cowboys, not in the Grand Entrée, tried to slow them down, but they just continued the race on down the road! The audience cheered and applauded WILDLY! They surely believed that they were getting their money's worth and THIS was just the beginning of the show!

I didn't see anyone injured from the ruckus and felt so relieved. Montie, who was in the announcer's booth, broadcasted there would be a short intermission. He quickly arranged for the wranglers to round up the unlucky riders with their racing mounts. It took a while for the horses and riders to calm down. Even though the riders were reluctant to remount these horses, they knew they had to for "the show must go on".

Dressed in my western leather outfit, I rode on the stagecoach pulled by a team of mules into the arena, circled once, and stopped. I got out displaying my "Miss Wild West," banner, and spun a loop with my rope to do the Flat Loop and Wedding Ring. After finishing, I waved to the crowd, climbed back into the stagecoach, and left the arena.

Next were the Native Americans who were to perform the Hoop Dance, the War Dance, and the Indian Prayer. Following them were Vi and John Brady, working their incredible act of whips, ropes and Boomerangs in the center of the arena. After the Bradys, the gunfight at the old corral and the saloon cancan dancers followed in the schedule. My Paneola Cowgirl act was to follow the cancan dancers. As the stage rolled to a stop, I leapt out the coach door, and rushed to the dressing room to change into my Hawaiian outfit. I knew I needed help with the grass shirt that had ties on the sides, the top and headpiece tying from the back, plus still needed to grab the extra props for my dance. With my heart pounding hard from the pressure to be on time, I felt a rush of panic, excitement, and nausea, all mixed up together as I ran out to the center of the arena. I had just enough time to kick off the shoes I was wearing before I heard my music begin and I started the dance routine barefooted. I felt the crowd staring at me as if they had never seen anything like this before. This experience felt especially strange as I was the only one in the arena performing! After my dance was completed, I jammed on my shoes and quickly exited the arena. As I charged into the dressing room to change into my next costume, Vi Brady was there and gave me words of encouragement expressing she had heard the crowd applauding, so they must have liked my act!

The show continued with trick riders, Roman Riders, and the Indians "attacking" the covered wagons.

I finished dressing in my western outfit for the show finale and went back to the arena. Montie had arranged for me to walk to the center of the arena with a microphone to thank the crowd in Malaysian for coming to the show. Upon ending my speech, the crowd cheered, declaring their delight. The show was once again a success!

After completing my necessary post-show chores, I arrived back at my hotel room. I still had more chores to do before going to bed! I sure wasn't in the mood to do my laundry; I just wanted to go to bed! I had a choice: to wear dirty underwear tomorrow or wash my lingerie out in the bathroom sink tonight. Even though I was bone-weary, I decided I wanted clean under-things and washed my laundry.

Chapter 7

A New Locale

Last night was a single performance, so now we faced the exhausting task of not only repacking all our gear, but also returning any borrowed items or animals, and journey for a full day by bus with this being the longest day of travel thus far. At least we had three days of performances in the next town, Kota Bahru! As a safety precaution, and with the all-too-fresh memory of bumping into the guerrilla soldiers the preceding day, Montie had the caravan of props and wagons following close behind us.

After returning the racehorses to the farm, Montie firmly stated we were not going to ever use racehorses again. They were just too dangerous!

Long trips are boring and tedious, but the perception of distance can be shortened when there is something fun to do or something funny happens. Some of the performers on our bus had a little joke among themselves.

It was common knowledge that I loved peanuts, so someone conjured up a plan, whispering it among the schemers in the back of the bus (which were mostly the trick and Roman riders). One of those jokers informed me that Malaysia had "Peanut Trees". They would point to a distant grove of trees along the route stating these were 'Peanut Trees'. I was so excited! Perhaps Montie could pull over so I could pick some of this wonderful snack food!! I would really look and squint trying to see the peanuts hanging from the trees, but the trees were just far enough away that I couldn't see anything except green. I completely believed what they were telling me! I could hear their muffled voices talking around me on the bus, but did not understand that this was a joke and the joke was on me! Montie chuckled at the fun and even Vi had to smile about this prank. I would spot another similarly looking grove, inquiring, "Are those more peanut trees?" I kept pacing up and down the bus aisle, always alert for the possibility of a 'Peanut Tree' being close enough for us to possibly stop and pick some peanuts! Finally, the landscape changed enough so there were no more trees that looked like the Peanut trees, so the joking stopped. Thankfully, I finally felt I could sit down; I was so tired of pacing. But at least I had a chance to see a real live Peanut Tree!

Night had already fallen by the time we arrived at the town of Kota Bahru by the Thai border. The wranglers handled the few animals we had brought along, so the rest of us were able to go straight to the hotel to check in. I had been sharing a room since arriving in Malaysia, but this time I was able to have a room all to myself. I was really surprised to see the bathroom in my room, since we were so deep in the jungle in such a small village. Taking a shower was going to be a real adventure, though, since the showerhead was directly over the toilet!

Since our arrival was so late in Kota Bahru (we hadn't stopped for a meal since lunch) and the trip had been hot and long, all we wanted to do was eat and go to bed. We discovered while checking in the lobby of the hotel for our rooms that the hotel restaurant had closed early, so we were forced to walk to another restaurant. The sidewalks were filthy since the streets were just dirt. While walking, all of us could see young and old with deformed bodies begging for money on the street. My heart broke for all those poor people! I noticed a little girl beggar and decided to give to her all the change I had in my pocket. Montie noticed my action, so I turned to him asking why there were so many deformed people. To make money for the family, mothers would strap their stomachs while they were pregnant with one of their children, thus forcing a deformity when the baby was born. When work was not to be found for any member of the family, the deformed family member begging guaranteed the family some sort of income.

We kept walking, crossing over a small bridge following the directions of the clerk of our hotel. Something jumped out in front of me, scaring me so much I screamed! In the dark, I could only make out the form of some large cat-like animal that had charged across my path. "What was that?" I asked. "Was that a very large cat?"
"No," Montie chuckled, "That was a rat!" The experience was such a surprise and the animal so large that I was shaking badly from what just happened and could barely continue walking! Eewww!!

I was still so very upset from the incident that when we arrived at the restaurant I found I really wasn't very hungry. We couldn't really read the menu as it was totally in Malaysian, so Montie ordered the food for all of us. He ordered "Masi Goreng" which is a rice dish. He informed us not to eat outside the hotel while in Malaysia, as most of the meat in the street stands and restaurants are dog, cat or horsemeat. Y-U-C-K!!!
I do NOT like rats, snakes, and bugs at all, because they really disgust me and scare me! Fast, slimy, icky things that can bite and hurt, that is why I don't like them. So when we

went back outside, I stayed very close to Montie as we walked back to the hotel. I really needed a good night sleep, but that whole night all I did was toss and turn, because of nightmares about eating dogs, cats, and horses, the crippled children on the streets, and the very large cat-rat animals.

The next morning we were feeling very tense as we went to the arena because we saw some Communist soldiers coming into town. They wore belts of bullets across their chests, carrying rifles and pistols, walking towards our hotel and later around the show arena. Not only were these soldiers scary because they carried these weapons, but we weren't sure if they would pick someone from our troupe to take as a hostage! All of us were looking out for each other, keeping watch so no one would just "disappear".

I had an interview with the reporter of the local newspaper at two o'clock pm. I stayed in the hotel to give the interview, because of the soldiers outside. The interview was to announce show times and show content, so this was nothing new to me. After the interview, I had to work on a new speech for the show. About an hour later, as I walked to the arena, about four blocks from the hotel, I kept looking around, keeping watch for any soldiers. I didn't wear my cowboy clothes or hat, just tried to blend in as much as a blonde American could, just so the soldiers would not notice me! Not only did I keep watch for the soldiers, but also those nasty, huge cat-rats! Montie told me the rats only came out at night, but I still kept a watchful eye out for one!
The show performers that day had found trail-ride horses at nearby ranches and were overjoyed they were not racehorses.

People in town were curious, coming out to watch the performers as they practiced inside the arena and out. The bleachers were "open", so folks could peek through the seat backs to catch a glimpse of the activities. Montie had no problem with the curious and "peekers", because they would eventually go back into town to tell their family and friends about what was seen which meant possibly more ticket sales. This was definitely free advertisement! Vi and John Brady decided to have a short practice while these town "spies" were out. I was trying to get up the nerve to ask John or Vi to show me a new rope trick. I could never understand why a performer would stop practicing his or her rope tricks when I was around. John and Vi told me that show people don't want anyone to watch them. Even teaching someone the trade was considered taboo, because, even as hard as it is to learn, that person being trained might steal the "teacher's" act. Then Vi turned to John asking if he would teach me a rope trick. WOW, I couldn't believe it! After all that was just told to me about how secretive show people were, this wonderful couple would even consider helping me?! I snatched up my rope, looking expectantly to John and anticipating what would happen next. The only problem I had to face was John was right handed and I was left, so I had to figure out how to spin the rope opposite to him. He demonstrated the Spoke Hop with the Flat Loop only once.

"Is that it?" I said.

"Yep, now you need to put the practice time in to do the trick," he flatly stated.

So, I turned the rest of the afternoon into a practice session with my rope. If I had to become skilled at this trick with the right hand first, I determined in my mind I would! First I tried the trick with my right hand and after an exhausting couple of hours, I finally figured how to step in and out of the loop without stepping on the rope. Now I attempted this trick with my left hand, but with the same problem... stepping on the rope! I labored all afternoon, sometimes with tears in my eyes, until very late. More times than not, I stepped on the rope, but at least I did the trick right a few times and had put in some serious practice!

Word sure did get out about the Wild West Show being in town! The tickets were selling fast and furious! I had just one more day to learn my Malaysian speech, since tomorrow was the opening show. Speaking Malaysian was just not easy for me! Montie had asked me to also end the show with a few words to the crowd in both Malaysian and English. So now I had to learn several sentences for the beginning and for the end of the show!! On top of that, I was still trying to learn the Spoke Hop rope trick! Practice takes time and I only had one more day for practice on both my speeches and the rope trick! I did manage to correctly complete the Spoke Hop more than miss it, even adding a little hop to it which made it look polished!

Thursday was opening night for the show! We had more talent in our show than any of these Malaysian people who lived in this small village had ever seen in their lifetime! I could NOT believe the turnout for the show! The arena held a lot of people and it was FULL!

I was in full cowgirl costume standing by the stagecoach when I discovered I had forgotten my Miss Wild West sash. I dashed back to the dressing room, grabbed it and ran back to the stagecoach with only a couple of minutes to spare!

When the crowd saw "Buffalo Bill Cody" and the Grand Entrée, they roared their approval and applauded. After the Grand Entrée, the stagecoach entered the arena with me inside it waving through the window at the crowd as we circled once around the arena. Since Montie was very exacting about every part of the show, no one dared to add anything which he hadn't previously approved. I followed my "script" to almost the end, but added an additional rope trick. As I re-entered the stagecoach, I happened to look up to where Montie was positioned in the announcement booth and observed his look of disapproval as he shook his head. I then realized that my little extra trick took time away from another act within the show, since all acts were timed to end to the minute, so the show would always end on time. I apologized to him later, promising I wouldn't add anything new without first checking with him.

After using run-away race horses, these horses were working out just great for the trick riding, Roman Riding, and Jess Montana's horse catches. Of course, there was always potential for a few falls in a horse riding act but as far as the audience was concerned, those falls made the show more exciting! Unfortunately for the riders of the show, they had a tumble or two. Falls could lead to injury or death of the rider, so no one in the show was happy about those accidents, even though the crowd roared and applauded!

When I noticed the stunt show and cancan dancers were in the arena, I knew I had just enough time to get dressed for my Hawaiian act. As I walked to the middle of the arena and started dancing, I could hear I was SERIOUSLY out of rhythm with the music! Finally I caught up, ending the routine in sync with the music. When the dance was over, the crowd was THRILLED! I admit I was flattered they liked it, but this crowd seemed overly applauding, so much more vigorously than after any other acts. I just couldn't figure out why they acted so enthusiastically. I left the arena for the dressing room to change into my buckskin vest, skirt, blouse, hat and boots for the finale.

None of us were paying attention to the crowd during the finale of the show. We hadn't noticed it was slowly making its way down to the gates leading into the arena. After the finale, all the performers cleared the arena as I walked out to the center with my microphone for my closing speech. I was concentrating on the Malaysian words of my speech, when about half way through it, I noticed that everyone from the grandstands had broken through the gates and were running down into the arena towards me. The next thing I knew, I was surrounded by an enormous, excited, unrestrained crowd and I was the only performer in the arena! The crowd went from gathering around me to grabbing at me and tugging at my clothes in an effort to touch me! I couldn't respond fast enough to the actions! As people were pushing me down towards the ground and tearing at my clothes, I somehow remembered Montie telling me if I should ever got in a bad situation, just whistle the cowboy whistle or call 'HAYRUBE' on the microphone, which is a code for "HELP!" I was so desperate and frightened that I kept whistling and screaming 'HAYRUBE' over and over again. Hands were touching or grabbing me on all parts of my body, tearing strands of my blonde hair, even ripping at my

blouse, skirt and vest. I was on the ground, fearing that I would now be trampled and die! My western scarf and hat were ripped off me. All of a sudden, I saw the crowd parting on one side. In came Montie and a few cowboys on horseback! Somehow, I managed to struggle to my knees, then to stand up. As I frantically attempted to mount the back of his horse, the other cowboys kept circling around us to force the crowd back. Montie grabbed me, hauling me up onto the back of his horse, then we rode out of the arena with the cowboys following Montie to keep the out-of-control mob at bay.

The crowd continued to follow us as we rode out toward our dressing room/single-wide trailers. All I wanted to do was get as far away from that crowd as I could! All the performers and I were actually trapped in the dressing rooms/trailers for over an hour while the crowd dispersed and went home. I was so shaken up that it took me some time to figure out where I was! All the female performers in the dressing room/trailer came over either to reassure, encourage, or help me care for my wounds. I had a lot of facial bruises on both sides of my face with extensive scratches on my legs, arms, and neck.

After the crowd broke up and went home, we were able to leave the safety of the dressing rooms/trailers and board the buses to return to the hotel. On the bus, Montie explained that the reason the crowd acted the way it did was because these simple folks had never seen an American Show and all they wanted was to take a piece of something "special" home with them.

After we arrived at the hotel, the plan had been for all of us to go to dinner. Fortunately, the restaurant was inside the hotel! I really don't remember getting off of the bus and finding my way to the restaurant, but somehow I was sitting at a table. I did my best to remain cheerful, not saying anything about what had just happened and the performers were all very sensitive to my feelings, not mentioning anything either. I was hungry, but eating the meal was difficult, since I hurt from one end of my body to the other, literally aching from head to foot! I did manage to complete my meal, but by the meal's end, I began to wonder if I would be able to move to the elevator and then to my room. I SO hurt! I did manage to get into my room, but my wounds were so numerous and painful, I could not take a bath to get completely clean. All I could do was pat my arms and legs with a washrag, struggle into my pajamas, and crawl into bed.

For the second night in a row I had horrific nightmares, this time of hands grabbing and pulling me down to the ground. At about three in the morning, I called Montie in his room. I asked him if he would help me feel better by hypnotizing me so I could sleep. He came to my room, had me sit in a chair, close my eyes and count down from ten to one. I really don't remember anything except opening my eyes again and feeling better. Montie left and I went back to being relaxed, sleeping more peacefully the rest of the night. It looked like another sold-out show for both Friday and Saturday. Extra security men were hired to stand at the gates to keep the crowd under control. Montie decided to discontinue my speech at the end of the Wild West Show after what had happened the previous night. I spent a considerable amount of time trying to cover up my bruises on my face and legs with the heavy stage make-up used in the show. I tried to forget about what had happened to me in the arena the previous night, I just went out to do a good act - but I was so sore! I no longer had my banner, so getting off the stagecoach seemed almost a waste of time, but I came out in it, waving as always! Keeping my head down, not looking at the audience when I did my roping did help keep me focused to do an average job on my act. At the finish of this part of the show, I began to feel very nervous since I knew I was going to be the only one in the arena for the Hawaiian dance. When I walked out to the center of the arena, I told myself over and over not to look at the crowd. Arriving at the platform situated in the center of the arena, I took a deep breath and waited for the music to begin. I counted the beats, then began to dance. And dance I did . . . right off the two- inch platform stage into the dirt arena! Somehow, I managed not to fall, but stepped barefoot into some horse poop. Yuck!! I kept dancing, but I could feel the poop pushing-up, squishing between each toe as I moved. After I finished, I slipped on my thongs and ran out of the arena to the closest water faucet. It took forever to get the poop off my feet and, BOY, did I stink!

Chapter 8

On The Road... Again!

The next town on our tour was six hours down the road. Once on the bus, the cowboys pulled their guitars out to sing, while the rest of us read books, napped or gazed out the window to enjoy the scenery. Once the cowboys became tired of singing, Montie, who was the most bored, shouted out "Look, Chyrle, there's Peanut Trees!" Way off in the distance there was a grove of trees. Everyone laughed as I jumped up to see. I finally realized that maybe some of the people on the bus weren't telling me the truth. This suspicion was confirmed when I looked at Vi Brady who was shaking her head at me as if to say "No, there isn't such a thing as a "Peanut Tree". I later learned that peanuts grew beneath the ground from the roots of a peanut plant. I kept up the joke during this portion of the journey, since everyone was having such a good time and the traveling went by a lot quicker by playing along with the joke. I decided that even though the "laugh" was on me, I could laugh at myself, too! I just carried on like I believed them, not wanting to spoil the fun.

Our destination, Georgetown, finally came into view. This town is located on the island of Penang. After we dropped off the wagons and props at the show arena in town, our buses took us to the hotel.

The hotel was small, with fewer rooms than some other locations we stayed, so we had to double up in the rooms. It turned out Linda, one of the trick riders, was put in my room, which would make the stay very stressful. Simply put, Linda did not like me. I was never asked to join her "group" nor were any of the other riders encouraged to ask. If anything, she discouraged anyone from "the group" to associate with me. Try as I might to be pleasant and friendly with her, she would ignore any overtures for friendship, to the point that the whole group couldn't help but notice her ostracizing me. Everyone in the show knew that the REAL reason for her hostility was her jealousy of me. I had no show biz experience and she believed I was getting all the attention. I knew she was just hoping something humiliating would happen to me during the performance, so I would be embarrassed in front of the crowd and, perhaps, fired by Montie for doing a bad performance. So looking forward to bunking with Linda was not going to be a pleasant event! By the time we both settled into the room, we were so tired all either one of us could think about was sleep! Yeah for twin beds!!

Sightseeing and shopping were the order of the day! No practices, no setting up, just rest and relaxation were on the schedule for that day! I awoke late, so by the time I got dressed and made my way down to the main lobby - everyone had made their plans for the day. I decided to go shopping by myself.

The hotel was two blocks from the center of town where any shopping to be found was located. The streets were made of dirt. This made the man-made walkways dusty and dirty. I maneuvered watchfully, careful not to run into any 'cat-rats'. Scattered sporadically along walkways were deformed people begging for money, their faces reflecting sorrow and despair. It took all the strength I could muster not to help any of these sad people. But I had been warned by Montie not to help or I would be mobbed by all of those begging!

The first shop I encountered was made of rough-hewn wood, secure enough to keep out rain, but definitely not a plush shop from Rodeo Drive in Beverly Hills! Walls, ceiling and floors were unpainted. No carpets graced the floor or curtains in the windows, everything rough and functional. But the merchandise!! Riotous colors of gorgeous silks graced wood boards used for displaying these exquisite textiles. The fantastic array of hues and delicate dyes blurred my vision, so I no longer noticed the building, only the merchandise. I asked the closest clerk if a blouse like the one I was wearing could be made for me. The clerk reassured me that this was very doable, instructing me to please choose from the selection of silks at hand. As my eyes wandered throughout the shabby store, flitting from one delicate pattern to the next, trying to make my selection, he took my blouse measurements. I finally made my choice, difficult as it was! I was instructed to return within two hours. Upon my return, the blouse was complete, fitting comfortably – a perfect fit! This kind of workmanship was amazing, costing me only five American dollars! At that price and quality of construction, I ordered two more western blouses and a pair of pants for the show. I hurried back to my room, retrieving the necessary costume items to be copied, returning as quickly back to the shop as I could. Later in the afternoon, I returned to the hotel with purchases in hand while wearing one of the blouses. I wished I had other family members' sizes, especially my mom's, so I could have something "special" to take back. Montie had already discovered more shops, informing the whole troupe of his discovery. Added to that, I had come back wearing one of these hand-made items, so it was not a surprise that over the next few days everyone was having outfits made.

When Montie and the rest of us performers got to the arena the next morning, we were surprised and amazed. The structure was huge and well kept despite being deep in the jungle and far from any large city. The inside was well built and the floor made of tile. Badminton games were the main event held at this facility. But the horses and wagons couldn't negotiate such a slippery surface! Our Sponsors and Montie had to appeal to the Chamber of Commerce to gain permission to put dirt or sand in the arena. The approval process seemed to take such a long time, even though the elapsed time was about a day! We were all stuck, unable to practice or construct the necessary building props for our show until a decision about the floor was forthcoming from the town's officials.

Approval came and with it truckloads of sand and dirt were hauled in to spread around the arena flooring by our support crew. The only person who refused to work was a guy named Randy, whose wife was such a good trick rider that Montie couldn't leave her behind. She, however, wouldn't travel without her husband. The only time that anyone caught Randy in any kind of work was when he was working on Montie for his and his wife's paycheck! Randy's refusal was the last straw for Montie. He was furious! He didn't want the guy to travel with the show in the first place, but because of Randy's wife's insistence to bring along her dead-beat husband, Montie had to hire them both. With Randy being a complainer to boot, the decision to fire him was no longer a problem, since Montie had had more than enough! If Randy's wife left as well, Montie would just fill her spot with someone else. He was not going to be held "hostage" by this loathsome bum

any longer! So Randy was handed his airline ticket home. His wife would have to make a decision whether to stay or go with him.

For two days the trucks continued to bring sand and dirt into the arena. Opening night was one day off, but the arena remained only half-filled.

Before the show Friday night, Montie explained to all the performers that the center of the arena was still very slippery due to the thin layer of soil. There was not enough time to completely cover the floor with enough dirt for safe footing for the horses. "There is no time to waste complaining now. I expect everyone to be very careful. All the horse riding, wagons, and stagecoaches in the show will remain around the outer edge of the arena. Stay out of the center of the arena," he commanded. As always with every opening to our show, first in the arena were the horses for the Grand Entrée. Then 'Buffalo Bill Cody' on horseback followed with the stagecoach with "Miss Wild West" inside. I could tell by riding in the stagecoach that the horses were having trouble getting traction with the slippery dirt floor. I stepped out of the stagecoach onto the arena and walked carefully to a wood platform to do my trick roping. Then I returned to the stagecoach to exit the arena. As I ran into the dressing room to change outfits for my next performance, I felt deep down inside that this was going to be a dangerous show to put on. Watching the show from the sidelines, awaiting my next cue, I held my breath as the trick riders entered the arena. The first rider was the Roman Rider, followed by a trick rider who did the "One- Legged Stand", standing in the saddle of the horse as the horse ran around the arena.

As the rider completed to circle the arena once, the second rider rode out beginning to vault from one side of her horse to the other as it ran around the outside track of the arena. The next trick rider went under the neck of the horse as the horse was running full speed. The last run was the most dangerous and difficult trick to perform as the rider went under

the belly of the horse at full speed. I released my breath as this portion of the show completed with no injuries. The finale of the program was the Indian attack on the settlers in a wagon train with the mounted Calvary coming to "save the day". Some of the horseback riders and wagon drivers must not have been listening to Montie when he sternly stated to stay out of the center of the arena, for the center of the arena was where they headed! The horses slipped and went down. With the horses falling, the wagons turned over, creating complete pandemonium!

It was definitely a Wild West Show! The performers and horses had enough cuts and gashes, and were bleeding just as if they were attacked by a real frontier Indian tribe, straight from the 1800's! We had to stay focused on the show, even though a few performers were carried out on stretchers with the center still filled with broken wagons and horses being medically treated so they could be removed to the comfort of their individual stalls. From my vantage point just outside the arena by a gate entrance, I watched with a sick stomach as performers were moved directly into an ambulance to be transported to the local hospital.

After the show, we had five performers in the hospital, several broken wagons, and two horses that needed to be put down. I could see in Montie's eyes that he sure hated to do ANY more shows in that arena. Later in the evening we learned that only one of the performers would have to have some sort of surgery on her leg, but the other four performers could be released with only cuts that needed stitches.

Before the show Saturday night, Montie stressed the importance of staying out of the center of the arena. He had also decided to eliminate the Indian attack and Calvary charge, which was the finale of the show, due to the dangerous condition of the arena center. This time everyone listened, for the show went off with no injuries or accidents. Thank Heaven!

For the crew and performers alike, Sunday became an ordered day of rest. Montie told all of us at breakfast that Sonia, a sixteen-year-old Native American trick rider, who was still in the hospital, had crushed her ankle from the accident two nights before during the center arena disaster and would need to have surgery. She was being transported to a much larger hospital for the procedure, and then would fly home to recuperate, accompanied by her mother, one of the members of our troupe. We later learned she could never trick ride again.

Before we left town on Monday, Montie had begun the arduous task of removing the dirt out of the arena. In order to gain approval from the leaders of the town to fill the arena with soil before our show began, an agreement was signed by Mars Film, our sponsors, guaranteeing that the arena would be completely cleaned out at the end of the run of our show. Two days later the Championship Badminton Tournament was to be held at this location. Mars Film broke their agreement, leaving the soil in the arena, not arranging for any clean up, and departing with us on the same day. We found out later that the tournament had to be postponed for a week and a half to get the soil out. Worse, the arena floor was damaged by our wagons and horses and needed repair work completed before any further sports event could be hosted. This further delayed the tournament, making the town leaders plus the avid sports enthusiasts enraged!

Our journey continued on to the next town of Ipoh. It was raining and humid, so we left most of the props and wagon in their traveling containers to keep them as dry as possible. The horses and livestock were taken to the outdoor arena to be fed and bedded for the night. The hotel staff, anticipating our arrival, had dinner on the table waiting for us. The taste of the food was acceptable, but while we were dining we noticed small lizards running up and down the walls of the restaurant. We were told that the lizards were welcome, because they ate the insects that were such a problem in the Malaysian jungle. After dinner, we were assigned our rooms. This time I didn't have to share my room, which was a welcomed relief after bunking with Linda! My toilet worked, but the shower water wouldn't turn on, plus several lizards of various lengths were scurrying all over the walls, ceiling and inside the tub as well! I was almost happy to walk downstairs to take a shower! This was a very creepy experience!

That night with the light on by my bed I lay watching those lizards climb up and down the walls of my room and listened to the downpour of rain outside. I know I didn't sleep much that night, since I was scared that those nasty, disgusting reptiles would either fall on me from the ceiling or find their way into my bed! Eewwwwww!!!

Chapter 9

Water-Logged and Sick!

It looked like our stay was going to be a wet one, as it was still raining when I woke up. Exhausted and groggy from the lack of sleep, I first noticed the bedside lamp was still on. As I pondered why I left it on, I caught movement on the wall next to me! In a rush, the previous night's fears raced back into my mind. I flung the blankets from me, wondering if I were the only occupant in my bed! Nope, no lizards! After stopping to roughly shake and carefully inspect each boot by my bedside, I felt comfortable enough to slip into my footwear in preparation to visit the bathroom. Getting dressed was a real adventure! Each article of clothing had to be cautiously inspected to make sure there were no lizards. This methodical search added much time to my normal morning routine, making me later than usual for breakfast.

Montie was in the restaurant as I entered. He related that he had already been to the outdoor arena, finding it had about five inches of standing water on the arena surface with no sign of the rain ending any time soon! Montie's policy had always been that the "show must go on", unless, of course, there was no audience or the sponsors of the show decided to cancel it. The performers couldn't safely practice any stunts in the rain, so most of us just stayed around the hotel. The only ones who were forced to venture out in this dismal weather were the American Indians and the wranglers. The Indians had to set up Teepees with whatever other items needed in their portion of the show and the wranglers to care for the show stock.

Saturday dawned with even more rain; a heavy, steady stream of water pouring from the sky! The standing water on the arena floor was closer to eight inches, with a slimy, oozy, muddy base beneath! Tonight was to be our opening night in this location! We all wondered, some aloud, whether we were to perform in our good costumes in this deluge! These expensive outfits would be ruined if we did, not to mention all our smaller props and performance gear would be trashed as well.

The buses drove up to the hotel on schedule, dropping us off at the dressing rooms by the waterlogged arena. Montie met us at our dressing rooms, answering our complaints with a serious expression, emphatically stating that he expected us to perform, regardless of the weather! He would not even listen, let alone entertain the thought of canceling. The show would go on as scheduled, end of complaints and discussion.

I woke up feeling slightly nauseated, figuring my churning stomach was due to lack of sleep, the constant downpour of rain, maybe the food, but definitely because of those lizards! However, as the day wore on, the nausea increased, plus an ever-growing headache was now added to the lousy way I was feeling. Would I last through the show or fall flat on my face or worse from the fatigue and weakness that began to grab hold of me, intensifying with each passing minute?!

Somehow, I dressed for my ride into the arena via stagecoach. Umbrella in hand, I staggered over to where I was to meet the stage. Peering into the arena, I viewed just a handful of people huddled under the covered grand stands to see the show, rather than the usual, filled-to-capacity audience we had come to expect. Even with the downpour of rain, the arena surface a muddy mess with standing water everywhere, our sponsors, Mars Films, steadfastly insisted since there was an audience, the show would continue as planned.

What a ridiculous stand! Just reimburse those folks their money! But, no! The final word was that Mars Films demanded the show to continue!

The Native American Indians had already set up the Teepees, but with all the water and muck in the arena the Teepee poles couldn't support the weight of the canvas covering. The normally erect teepees were slouching down or completely flat on the muddy surface. There was just no way to secure the poles in the over-sodden soil of the arena to keep the heavy mud-and-water teepees upright! Just a few minutes before the show was to begin, Raszak from Mars Films decided to cancel. Whew!!

We were all so relieved! By now, I was seriously sick to my stomach with what I figured was the flu. I barely was able to climb onto the bus that would take us back to the hotel. Vi spotted me as I slouched down in the seat of the bus, looking miserable. She suggested that after we arrive at the hotel, I should go straight up to my room and she would follow with my gear. I was so relieved! The moment the bus stopped at the hotel, I staggered into the hotel, struggled up the stairs, and headed straight for the bathroom. Afterwards, I somehow managed to undress, wriggle into my nightgown, and climb into bed, keeping my boots right by my bedside in case I needed to make another mad dash to the bathroom. I laid my spinning head down on the pillow, not caring if there were any lizards that had somehow crawled beneath. As I lay on my side in misery, I gazed at the lizards climbing the wall, noticing for the first time small roach-like beetles scurrying across the bedroom floor! Being so focused on the lizards, I hadn't noticed anything else. The wet weather must have forced these insects to find a dryer place to live. Suddenly my stomach jumped and churned, forcing me to jump into my boots, just making it to the bathroom! Even in my state of misery, a humorous thought came to mind. Who would believe this scene! Here I am, camped in the bathroom, dressed in a nightgown and cowboy boots, sick as a dog, watching lizards scamper up and down the walls while cockroaches crawled over and under my boots! Boy, did I feel like all I wanted was my mom!! Again for a second night, I kept the light by my bedside burning, this time more for crossing to and from the bathroom rather than keeping track of lizards. Twelve trips from bed to the bathroom were made that night. More the ache of the fever that hit right after I had first arrived to my room than the fear of lizards finding their way into my bed kept me from falling into a sleep I so desperately needed.

At one point during the early dark hours of the morning, I happened to look up, noticing that now the lizards were on the ceiling directly over my bed. Holding my breath in fear, I watched in horror as gravity had its way, with a few of those gross things falling down onto my blankets! I screamed, frantically brushing and batting at them with a pillow as they landed, then scrambled to get away from my blows. Not only am I sick, running back and forth to the bathroom, achy from an accompanying fever, having to shake out my boots to keep the cockroaches out, but NOW kicking and swatting at stupid lizards falling from above. Yuck! Daylight just was not coming fast enough for me! I was forced to "make do" with a horrible situation until morning. Eww!!

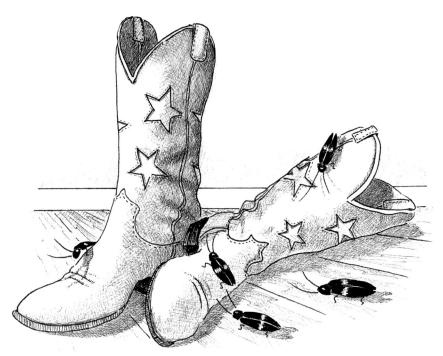

The rain had stopped sometime in the night with the sunshine breaking through my window the next morning and I found myself feeling better even though I had had little sleep. The fever had broken and my stomach was not lurching anymore. I was actually a bit hungry, although the thought of food still made me feel sick. Breakfast consisted of a piece of dry toast and weak tea. For lunch I had a bit more, but still went easy on my stomach. I did not want to repeat the agony I experienced the night before by overeating!

Since it had just stopped raining, everything was still drenched from the last few days of rain. The sponsors decided to allow us all a day off to give the outdoor arena time to dry out. Since the hotel was at the edge of town as was the arena, many of the performers decided to go into town, taking advantage of any good buys plus doing a bit of sightseeing. The temperature always felt humid, even when it didn't rain. I totally enjoyed laying by the pool on our day off, away from lizards and cockroaches to just REST! What a joy to finally sleep without fear of something crawling on me.

Later in the day, Raszak told Montie that the arena was still too muddy, that it would take too many days for it to dry out enough to be useable. So plans had been made for the show to move on to the next town eight hours away, where the tickets were selling quickly.

Monday morning came with the "time to hit the long trail" theme as we moved all our gear to the next town! Seven of us were asked by Montie to stay behind for that day. There was John and Vi Brady, a Native American Indian, Jones Banelly, who did the Hoop Dance, Montie, his son Jess, daughter, Kelly, and me. Montie needed to complete paperwork for the shows that were canceled, plus work on some promotional material for the upcoming show in the next town and just wanted us along for any preshow promotions. The plan was to complete the necessary work where we were while the show caravan traveled ahead, then, later that day, fly by plane to the next town, catching up and meeting the troupe at the sports arena that night for an eight pm show.

Gee, some time to clean my costumes and practice some roping! I was having difficulty with the "Pop Ups", a new rope trick, so this was an answer to prayer!

Chapter 10

On Our Own

Five pm rolled around with the seven of us meeting in the lobby of the hotel to leave for the airport. All of us were dressed casually as we carried our costumes for the plane ride to Johor Bahru. Many armed soldiers were visible when we arrived at the airport, since we were so close to the Thai border. I realized we had a lot of costumes and props for our different acts, so it would be a very full load for the small Cessna airplane! Montie, being a pilot himself in the United States, sat as a co-pilot, helping the pilot with preflight duties. Take off went well with the weather clear. I didn't say much during the ride, since I was very nervous, white-knuckling the armrest as we bumped down the runway and into the air. The light quickly disappeared since the hour was so late. There wasn't much to see out the window to keep my mind away from the fear of being in such a little plane so far off the ground. Our fight time was approximately one and a half hours in the air. Vi and John Brady chatted to each other in their wonderfully comforting Australian accent, occasionally including Jones Banelly in their conversation. Kelly and Jess sat back in the seat with their eyes closed. As I sat upright and stiff in my seat, I wondered if anyone was as scared as I was! But, no, everyone looked so relaxed! Towards the end of the flight, there was a bit of turbulence, making the plane bobble a bit, adding to my nervousness. We all made it in one piece, even though the landing strip had few lights and the plane bounced a bit upon landing.

It was now seven thirty pm. Since this was a larger airport, we were extremely surprised to find the whole terminal and surrounding area almost completely dark. No planes were taking off or landing. This seemed very strange! Since there was no other plane traffic, our plane taxied up to the main terminal. Even more curious, there were three vehicles traveling at a fairly fast rate, headed in our direction with their headlights glaring. The cars squealed to a stop directly next to the plane as we began to disembark, unloading our belongings. These were the taxicabs hired by Raszak for transporting us to the arena for our show tonight. The obviously nervous drivers motioned for us to come with them quickly. Montie was told by the pilot that the airport was closed, because of Communist troop activities.

The pilot began to translate into English what the drivers were saying in Malaysian. "The crowds are waiting for the show, they are getting upset, and no one has arrived yet!"

Where was the show caravan?! They should have already arrived and set up for the show! What happened to our performers? We had to start the show in half an hour, just the seven of us! We decided to hurriedly use the bathroom, hastily adding make-up and fixing our hair as we dashed back out the door.

Outside the terminal building, we saw armed soldiers positioned in strategic areas, observing us with hostile eyes. "Hurry," the taxi cab drivers said in Malaysian, pulling on us toward the cars, "HURRY! HURRY!" Vi and I jumped into the back seat of one taxi, while the others jumped into the other two. The cabs screeched out of the darkened airport terminal area and hurtled down the two-lane road. By the strained tone of our taxi cab driver's rapid-fire conversation on the business walky-talky and his frantic driving, we could tell he was very nervous.

In the back seat of the bounding taxi, Vi and I tried to dress for the show, while the cab jerked us from side to side as it flew around curves and hurtled up and down hills on the unevenly paved road. As I struggled to put on my false eyelashes, the ride reminded me of a roller coaster ride of extremely high speeds! I started getting a little sick from all the jumping around. Vi and I eventually managed to get on our costumes, although the fake eyelashes really never did get put on correctly!

Cresting a large hill, we discovered our roller coaster of a taxicab ride had almost come to an end. Forest gave way to a momentary unobstructed view of the valley below, allowing us to catch from almost a half-mile away a quick look at the stadium where we were to perform. The structure was a large, open, well-lit sport complex packed with people who must have come for miles just to see this show! We just couldn't believe our eyes! "From where did all these people come?" Vi and I voiced in astonishment. In the frantic, after-dark drive from the airport, bouncing around inside the taxi like rubber balls attempting to dress for the show, we really hadn't had time to notice anything, except a narrow, graveled road with the occasional small farm. And no sign of our caravan!

What was Montie thinking of this situation? He had crested the hill first in the front taxicab. He must be frantic! I know I was!! As we skidded to a stop in near one of the back exits, throwing gravel in all directions, we noticed patrons were either angrily standing around, near the ticket booths or angrily leaving the stadium area. These folks had been sitting or standing in the grand stands for an unknown amount of time for the show to begin. They obviously felt cheated by having to wait so long and wanted their money back! What were we to do without the props, animals, wagons and other performers that were right now nowhere in sight?!

Montie quickly assembled all of us in a huddle to focus on his plan of action. Above the din of angry voices and stomping feet demanding the promised show, Montie calmly reminded us the "SHOW MUST GO ON" with or without all of the props, wagons and everything else. Montie quickly dashed up to the announcer's booth to reassure the agitated crowd, speaking in both English and Malaysian that this show would begin in fifteen minutes, asking for the crowd's patience. He sprinted back down the stairs, yelling for all the stage help within earshot to gather around him. These were the stadium crew, the men who maintained the arena. Being locals, these men would know where horses and other needed livestock might be found close to this structure and be available quickly. "We have no time to waste," stated Montie to these men in Malaysian. "Where can we get horses and goats?" The stagehands promptly volunteered to go see what they could find, hurriedly scattering in the dark in every direction.

The people in the grand stands began anew to chant loudly, stomping their feet in agitation to get the show started. One of the remaining stagehands frantically directed the six of us to the dressing room. We all took a corner of the room, laying out costumes, make-up, and props as the order of the show dictated. Montie had just roughly scrawled out the show's 'order of appearance' on scratch paper, giving it to a stagehand who hastily delivered it to us. Montie had already disappeared back into the announcer booth to update and reassure the crowd that the show was about to begin, with the interpreter translating it into Malaysian.

The stage help had returned in less time than anticipated, bringing with them one ancient, sway-backed horse and 3 goats that some farmer unknowingly lent. The horse looked to be on its last legs, having been found in an isolated pasture. The poor old horse was hurriedly saddled up for probably a first adventure of its very long life!

Now, just imagine this picture! A stadium that could probably seat fifty thousand people, every seat taken with folks sitting on the aisle steps or standing in the back rows, all waiting to see our Wild West Show presently consisting of only seven performers, just one old horse, three goats, nothing else!! No wagons, stagecoach, music, Indian Tee-Pees, or anything else! What a mess! Luckily for us, Montie had packed some recorded music we could use for some of the acts.

First act out was the trick ropers. With no plywood platforms, like we had in previous shows, John, Vi, Kelly, Jess, and I spaced ourselves so the crowd could get a look as we attempted to spin rope loops, while missing the soft dirt underfoot. Without spotlights, the audience must have had a difficult time seeing us! We must have looked like ants to the crowd! By the way, due to that soft dirt, spinning loops to hop into just didn't happen! I didn't even try to count how many times that dirt snarled my loop! Adding to that problem, I could only try to do the Wedding Ring loop or the Flat Loop (that spins very close to the ground).   I stopped after a few unsuccessful attempts. I learned real quick that I would have to keep my rope up and away from the two foot dirt in the arena or the loop would snag and stop. I played it safe, performing only the Cowboy's Wedding Ring. No spoke hops or hand changing with the rope tonight! The rowdy crowd calmed down considerably just to see some action in the arena.

79

After the trick roping, Montie announced Jones Benally and his Indian Hoop Dance. As good as Jones was with his performance that evening, the crowd wasn't that entertained seeing only just one Native American Indian performing. They started stamping their feet again as if to say, "Where was the Wild West Show we had heard so much about?" Setting up back behind the stage was John Brady saddling that old nag of a horse. He was borrowing a western saddle that had been packed in the plane. Again, try to imagine a fellow, who normally let the younger riders do the trick riding stunts, astride a very old sway-back horse who seemed barely able to trot into this over-packed stadium. Usually there were at least six to eight trick riders performing on young horses running at top speed for a crowd this size! This old horse had no idea what she was about to experience! John smacked the old horse in the ribs with the heel of his boots as they entered the arena to get her moving out of that slow trot. John actually got her into what could be loosely called a run! What a sight to see! It was as if the old swayback horse was running in slow motion. The old gal hadn't moved that fast in years. Bless her heart, she was giving all she could and so was John! Montie introduced John as he circled around the arena of the stadium. The first run John did was a side-to-side vault. Then the second run John did the dead man's drag.

By the third turn around the arena, this old horse was sweating heavily and breathing hard! John motioned to Montie in the announcer's stand that this would be her last run. John exited the arena and took the old girl out to cool her down and gave her a big hug as if to say, "You're a GOOD OLD GAL! You did the very best you could! Now you can retire to the pasture for the last of your years!"

As the poor old gal was departing the arena, the next scheduled event was my "Panola Cowgirl" routine and I was ready and waiting in the wings as the pair left.

The single changing room left us performers with absolutely no privacy. Having to completely change out of my cowgirl outfit into a barely-covering top and full grass skirt, I couldn't worry about getting embarrassed while fully changing into the next outfit. Besides, with only seven of us in the show, we were much too busy getting dressed for our each scheduled event to take the time to sneak any kind of "looks".

I didn't have any recorded music with me for my routine, so I had to count on Montie for support. As I walked to center of the arena, Montie began to play his guitar, trying to make it sound like a Hawaiian Ukulele. It sounded so comical! Here is a slow drawling cowboy, whose voice is best suited to slow country music, and he was desperately trying to keep up his singing to the fast Hawaiian beat. Smiling during the performance was easy, but I had to force myself to stay focused on my dancing, so I wouldn't stop dancing and double over in laughter!

With no platform to dance on and no spotlight to mark my location for the crowd, I walked to the center of the arena and just kept my eyes closed to concentrate on the music playing over the sound system and my performance. During these complicated dances, I had to add turns to my steps in my routine, so I would be facing every side of the arena and the audience. With the soft dirt and these added movements, the dance steps became very difficult to complete. In addition, I seriously doubted I was holding anyone's attention during my whole routine, since I didn't think anyone could see me. When the last dance was completed, the applause was deafening! I guess I WAS seen by all!

Fear had followed me into this huge stadium arena. After that awful time in a previous show with the huge crowd trying to "tear" me apart, I was very worried that the crowd might rush down onto the field again and this time I was truly by myself. There were not enough performers and no horses to come to my rescue should the crowd come down to the arena. Thank heavens, the crowd stayed in their seats, even after I left!

As I dashed back to the dressing room to change again to my western costume, Vi and John Brady's act was introduced. Being professionals in every sense of the word, they had their own large mat for their different acts, plus their own music, both of which were always in their possession. The stage crew and John had just completed the pre-staging of the mat and some of the equipment needed for their performances with rope, Australian Bull and Stock Whips and boomerangs as I was departing the arena. The couple was flawless in every act they performed, including their entry and exit! John flung the boomerang over the audience heads, the thrumming whir was heard over the excited cries of the multitude. Vi flicked a button off John's tongue, then John snapped a bull whip at Vi's waist, removing her long, flowing skirt to reveal an exquisitely decorated leotard bottom. The throng roared its approval as their act ended and they departed!

Montie's next act on this impromptu schedule was a sing along. As each performer went out, we were handed a microphone, instructed to stand in the middle of the arena face different sections of the grand stands and follow Montie's lead. Montie had a wonderful, full singing cowboy-type voice, sounding a lot like Roy Rogers. This was my first experience singing in front of an audience! As I sang the first few bars of the first song, the rest of the performers realized that I just couldn't sing. The microphone was promptly removed from me, with the music continuing. We sang "You are My Sunshine", "Don't Fence Me In", "Home on the Range" and "San Antonio Rose". I just mouthed the words for the remainder of this act.

After the sing along and as we were departing the arena, we heard Montie over the loud speaker say, "Ladies and Gentlemen, boys and girls, we will be back in fifteen minutes after the intermission for the second half of the show." We couldn't believe what we were hearing! We had done all the acts that the seven of us could do! What was left?! Montie met us at the dressing room. "Okay," he said, "we need to come up with the second half of the show. I will be back in ten minutes expecting to hear your ideas." Our ideas?!!

Montie departed to talk to our sponsor's representative, plus find out the approximate location of the caravan of performers and props. While Montie was gone, we all racked our brains to dream up the second half of the show.

One person came up with The Native American Indian Prayer and Round Dance possibility. No one else had any ideas!

There was still NO sign of our traveling show and now we had 5 minutes before the second half of the show was to begin!

When Montie returned to our dressing room, he had a few more ideas of his own for the second part of the show, which included the goats that had been 'borrowed" with the horse. These three very skinny goats had no WAY of knowing what was going to happen to them! The rumbling and foot stomping in the grand stand was telling us the restless crowd wanted the second half of the show to begin. I wasn't going to get my costumes dirty for this next creative event that Montie came up with, a goat-tying event, so I hurried to change into my blue jeans, t-shirt, old boots and cowboy hat. Montie had already gone out ahead of us to pick twelve people out of the audience to participate while I was changing. We would offer a cash prize to the winner. Montie hollered, "Let the fun begin!" We had to show the volunteers how to play before they could participate. I, myself, really didn't know how to play the game, so I watched and listened carefully as Montie explained to the audience from the announcer's booth what was to happen! There were three teams, four people per team. Montie called "On your mark, get set, go!" I ran in ankle high dirt with my teammates down to the end of the arena where our goat was standing. When the goat saw us charging toward him, he took off running. I tried to block the goat before he had a chance to get away, but each member on our team missed catching him and the goat ran to the far end of the arena, shaking his head and shivering.

Someone seriously needed to explain the concept of goat tying to the volunteers on my team, because all they did was follow me around with their ropes. At one point, I bent over to pick up my rope and one volunteer came straight for me as if to lasso me instead of the goat! I thought this could really get out of hand! We eventually caught our goat, looping the rope around his neck, heading towards the finish line. Too late! The horn sounded, declaring there was a winner! We did three more goat tying events and gave away more cash prizes. I was exhausted after running all over the arena in ankle-high dirt for the last three events. I couldn't imagine doing any more of the show without the caravan here!

Just as we were about ready to give up because we were all exhausted, I happened to glance over at the main gate and spotted a couple of vehicles from our caravan driving by the gate opening. "They're here!" I screamed to all the performers that were within earshot. Performers' heads turned questioningly towards me, then their eyes followed to where I was pointing. Within a few minutes Montie was heard over the P.A. system announcing the arrival of the rest of the caravan, explaining to the audience that there would be a brief intermission while the cast and crew set up for the rest of the show. He further explained to the crowd that the show would last extra hour for all. The whole cast that had just arrived was exhausted from the journey, but sprang into action despite the road weariness. Wranglers hurried to saddle up horses brought from the last show, the wagons and stagecoach were quickly hitched up, and the performers jumped into their costumes to put on the BEST SHOW EVER for the stadium crowd!

Our small team of seven performers huddled in a corner, hugging each other in relief and delight. We had kept the multitude entertained until our "troops" had arrived! We were equally relieved that now we would not be responsible for what could be loosely called the "rest of the show". Montie came back down briefly to inform us that we would not have to perform anymore tonight. He felt we had done enough. We still went into the dressing rooms to assist with costumes and props, even though no one expected us to help. Later, in bed reflecting over the day, I felt really good about what we had accomplished with improvisation to continue the show and not disappoint the audience. Somehow we had pulled it off!

After the show that night, Montie commented to everyone, "Never say, it is impossible to put on a Wild West Show with only seven people, because we proved IT IS POSSIBLE!" The next night, the audience was even larger than the previous night. Some funny incidents happened with some of the announcers of our show. Montie had to prepare a written script for each performance in each town we visited, where it would then be translated in Malaysian for the crowd to hear. The translation from English into Malaysian for each act didn't translate literally. I learned from our show interpreter later how the performance descriptions sounded to the audience. For example, "Trick

Roping" translated into "The Fantastic Magical Hanging," and 'Deadwood Stage' translated to "The Dry Branch Stage." I had wondered why at times during our performances as I gazed on audience faces, these people looked at each other with bewilderment!

Chapter 11

New Horizons

The final show had been completed and our travels through Malaysia had come to an end as we circled back to the capital, Kuala Lumpur. Our tour back was only a day's journey. While on the bus ride that day, the performers confessed to me that they had been pulling my leg about peanut trees and that peanuts grow on the roots of the peanut plant. I kinda figured that out earlier in our travels, I told them, because of the laughter generated when I would get excited seeing a Peanut Tree.

We arrived back in Kuala Lumpur that evening around six pm. After we dropped off the caravan of wagons and props at a Mars Film storage facility, we went to the hotel to check in. This was the same hotel we had stayed at the beginning of the trip where I did my very first performance in their lounge. We were all so hungry that we went straight down to the dining room. Everyone was enthusiastic about the idea of having the next day off.

After our meal, Montie invited some of us to join him in the lounge to watch the lounge show. When we walked in, Montie had ordered all of us non-alcoholic drinks. During the entire tour, Montie had some basic social rules for the troupe and the most strictly enforced rule was absolutely NO alcohol consumption. To break this rule meant immediate dismissal and a quick trip home. I had a "Roy Rogers" drink (cherry Coca Cola), and sat back to enjoy the lounge show.

From the first time I had met him, I admired Montie for his quick thinking, the ability to handle any situation thrown at him, being kind to all, and being compassionate. For these reasons, I had a crush on him and had been trying to come up with a way to tell him my feelings, but there never seemed to be an appropriate time. Plus I struggled with the reasoning of whether this was a "right and proper" feeling I was experiencing. There just never seemed to be a private time to talk with him, since he was never alone with all the responsibilities he had. The only person who knew how I felt was Vi Brady, as we talked a lot during our extensive travels through Malaysia. She encouraged me to pursue him, since he was single and believed we would be a good 'match'. Sitting in the lounge next to him having such a great time enjoying the show and a sweet drink, I reached my hand over to his hand, held it and looked him in the eyes, telling him I liked him. He smiled and said, "I like you too, Chyrle." He didn't understand how deeply I felt! After the show had ended, I left for my room, feeling frustrated over my lack of words to him and the disappointment of his reaction. During the night, I dreamt that Montie and I were married. We had a huge cowboy wedding, riding off on our horses into the sunset, living happily ever after. This was an infatuation, I realized, and not true love. The feelings I was feeling were reasonable, since this kind, knowledgeable man rescued me from several bad situations and even saved my life – just like a patient falls in love with the doctor who saved the patient's life!

Tuesday morning woke me by a phone ringing in my ear at eight am, startling me out of my sweet dream. Vi called to see if I wanted to join John and her to go sightseeing on our day off. I eagerly agreed, arranging to meet downstairs in the lobby at nine am to first have some breakfast, and then to take a cab to the Batu Caves. These caves were in a massive limestone outcrop with a gargantuan interior that served as home to Hindu deities. This was such an amazing sight! I thought I was in shape, but after climbing up two hundred steps and back down again from the caves I was exhausted! I was very thankful we had a cab to drive us back to the hotel! When we got back, I shared with the other performers about our exciting day.

While the performers were out shopping or sightseeing, Montie was taking care of business and making plans for our departures for the next day. Our next stop was Singapore. The plan was the performers were to take a commercial flight to Singapore, while all the Wild West wagons, stagecoach and props would be sent unescorted in a large military-type freight airline a few days later. The one thing we discovered in Malaysia was that when we entered a new town, the police were really fussy about the weapons we brought with us for the show. All our western guns and rifles were identical to the real rifles used in the Old Wild West days, but we used blanks for bullets. In some locations, it would take between five to seven days to get the guns out of customs. Montie wasn't going to deal with customs in Singapore, so he just smuggled them across the border.

After lunch Wednesday, we all met down in the main lobby to ride buses for our departure to the airport. I was exceedingly excited to go to Singapore, since I had read about this cosmopolitan city in travel guidebooks and school textbooks. We were all ready to go when we noticed that a few of the Native American Indians were missing. I glanced towards Montie, noticing his worried expression. Montie stepped over to a phone, calling their room, but no one answered. "Well," he said, "Maybe they will meet us at the airport." Every time the troupe had to travel anywhere, Montie always had to remind the Native American Indians to be ready and waiting two hours earlier than departure time, since they were never on time! We couldn't afford to have them miss the flight to Singapore.

We arrived at the airport and began to line up to board our flight. Montie kept a sharp eye for the lagging few as he passed out the plane tickets. Just before the doors of the plane shut, Montie and the three stragglers boarded the plane. That was a relief! Since we had no personal cell phones in those days, we had no way to contact these guys or know what was happening. Montie was quite agitated by the stress from waiting for these few and groused at the Native Americans NOT to let THAT happen again.

I always ask for the aisle seat on the planes, because of my long legs. This flight offered free beverages and a small selection of dinners. Even though this would be a short flight, only four hours, I fidgeted in my seat in excitement

Chyrle Bacon

89

in anticipation of visiting Singapore! This was a very modern city with an enormous import and export trade from its seaports, plus most of the people spoke English. I was really looking forward to not having to quickly learn a new language. Upon our arrival at the Singapore's airport, Montie encountered a huge problem at customs. We learned that Singapore law did not allow men to enter the country with long hair. All of our Native American Indian men had long braided hair, as was the custom of their tribe. Since we were not prepared for this problem, Montie had to quickly and painstakingly explain to the authorities the reason the Native American men wore their hair so long, while the rest of us waited. Montie, being the expert he was at negotiating, finally convinced the officers that our Native Americans could keep their long braids if they tucked their braids up in their softball caps or cowboy hats while they were out in public. If these men agreed to this rule, they would be able to enter the country. Only for the Wild West Show would they be able to let their braids down in the public view.

We boarded buses for transport from the airport to the hotel. The first thing I did upon arriving in my room was separate my laundry into two piles: clean and dirty. I took the dirty clothes to the hotel laundry room for washing. While I hung around waiting for the washer and dryer to finish, I practiced my rope tricks in the hallway. A few people gathered to watch my practice session. Since I had an audience, I did a couple of tricks, just to impress the watchers. Applause followed my short routine. The small crowd realized I had completed my "show" and moved on.
Now I could begin to practice the harder rope tricks, not wanting anyone watching as I was sure I would make mistakes. The rope trick that was giving me the most trouble was called Butterflies.

Over and over I practiced, but always seemed to lose the loop after the third spin. I kept trying until I decided I definitely needed someone to 'spot' me to see what I was doing wrong. When I finished my laundry, I walked back to my hotel room. As I opened the door, the message light on the phone was blinking. Montie had left a message informing me that we all had the next two days off. He said that he wanted to take our group on a bay cruise around the bay of Singapore. I knew there was no way I was going to miss this adventure! I decided to go to bed early. I wanted to be rested and look great the next day for the sightseeing cruise!

I must have been very tired, for the next morning I was suddenly awakened by someone frantically knocking at my bedroom door. "Let's go!" someone yelled through the door," You're going to miss the bus!" Oh no, it was nine am and I had overslept! I got dressed as fast as I could, grabbed some make-up and a jacket, hurrying down to the front lobby where everyone was waiting on the bus. As I climbed on, Vi handed me a banana, since I had completely missed breakfast and she knew I would be hungry. As the bus pulled out of the parking lot, I worked to pull myself together, putting make-up on and combing my hair. It was still early for morning, but already hot and humid! When we arrived at the dock to board the cruise boat, there were actually two seats left that were together at the front of the boat. Montie sat down next to the vacant seat, I sat next to him. That day he didn't have business on his mind, so he was relaxed and so much fun to be around! As I sat in my seat, I realized the cruise director was speaking in English, pointing out the Singapore Bay's history. The boat visited nearby rice paddies, where farmers were working in ankle deep water on their plants. The two or three hour tour also included skyscrapers perched on the water's edge. Following the bay, the tour continued revealing different boat types, from stylish transports to makeshift Junks, a type of houseboat. The water was constantly churned up by bay activity, bumping and rolling our craft around enough to upset some of the sightseers' stomachs. Everywhere there was activity! Despite how much business this bay sees each day, the view was still breath-taking!

After we disembarked from the tour ship, our bus took us to the Raffles Hotel where the famous "Singapore Sling" cocktail was introduced. Since this was a traditional Singapore beverage, we were 'allowed' this one strong drink. We all sat in the beautiful gardens of the hotel that late afternoon and enjoyed our treat. It was delicious! I wondered if life could get any better than this?! I secretively pinched myself to make sure this wasn't a dream! First the cruise, then this gorgeous garden! I had an enjoyable time. After enjoying our drink, we headed back to the hotel where we were staying.

Chapter 12

A Good Friend, A Spa Treatment & A Nasty Prank

Throughout our journey in Malaysia, Vi Brady and I had established a solid friendship. Vi had great stage presence, was exacting in her performances so they were always flawless, kept herself in great physical shape, and I firmly believed she was just one very classy lady!

She quietly lamented to me that this Malaysian back-country tour had really trashed her hair and skin, suggesting that we should – first chance we could – go to a health spa for some well-earned sprucing up. I eagerly agreed with her! My skin felt like sandpaper from the sun and heat, my nails looked awful, and my hair was so dry it felt fried! When we arrived at our hotel, the first thing we did was look for a spa, finding one right on the property! Hurrah!! We couldn't make that appointment fast enough for an "all over", from head-to-toe spa treatment! What a day! I was treated like a queen!

John & Vi Brady

After spending the entire day at the spa, Vi and I had an early dinner together. I noticed Vi carefully watched everything she ate, eating very healthy foods that helped to keep her slim and trim. Now I understood how she always stayed looking so good! She didn't just exercise to keep in shape, but also watched what she ate. All of this was important, since our costumes were very form-fitting and expensive! Not one of us could just go buy another pair of pants to go with the costume jacket, since all these costumes were specially made, very expensive and one-of-a-kind!

After breakfast on Saturday, several of us performers were scheduled to visit a couple of children's hospitals. These poor little ones, for various major health reasons, could not attend our shows, so we brought the show to them! Of course, the stagecoach and wagons couldn't be brought, but we would do rope tricks and sing cowboy songs while in full costume. The eyes of these children shone with excitement! They laughed and cheered for us as we performed our shortened acts. They even became part of the action, spinning a small rope made especially for each child that could manage the activity. This benefit always brought such a warm feeling to my heart!

With the show opening in a short few days, I wondered if the ticket sales where as promising as Malaysia. As the PR person, I had only one interview with a local television station scheduled at the outdoor show arena on Wednesday. The weather forecast was rain straight through the weekend.

I was on my own for the television interview at the arena which was scheduled for two pm that day. The performers would be practicing there at the same time I had the interview. I arrived early, wearing my nice butterfly costume and had two ropes with me. When the reporters showed up, we walked around the old frontier town scene, taking pictures and working with me to feel at ease with the television camera. Then one of the reporters asked if I could get on a horse. The trick rider, Linda, who was so jealous of me, heard our conversation. She spoke up saying, "Sure, we can get a horse for Chyrle."

"Uh, oh!" I groaned to myself.

Since I couldn't ride a horse and had no experience with these creatures, Montie only allowed me to ride the gentlest ones. But this time Montie wasn't there to help pick out a horse for me, as he always did in the past. Not wanting to embarrass myself by saying I couldn't ride and knowing how mean she could be, I waited in dread for Linda to bring back the horse she had chosen. She came back leading the saddled, high-spirited white stallion of the guy who performed 'Wild Bill Cody' in our show and she was having a difficult time controlling this horse. She wasn't about to ride in to where we were waiting with this frisky stallion which had not been exercised for several days.

Spying this magnificent creature, the reporters became more enthusiastic about the rest of this once slow-moving interview, requesting I stand in front of the stallion holding his reins while they snapped some pictures. Even as I stood stock still in fright, faking the best smile I could muster, I prayed that this beast would behave and not rear or jump, knocking me to the ground and dragging me around, or worse, trample me! Perhaps no one will ask me to mount this excited creature! Beads of perspiration formed on my forehead as the photographers continued to snap pictures. Just as I thought we were done, Linda piped up with "Why don't you all get some pictures on the horse, Chyrle?" Of course, the reporters all thought that was a super idea! I wanted to glare at Linda for her mean-spirited suggestion, but had to keep smiling as I lifted a trembling left foot into the stirrup and snatched the horse's reins from the Linda's grasp. I mounted the stallion, sitting straight in the saddle. The stirrups were adjusted for another rider, but I had no experience in altering them, so left them alone. My legs looked rather odd, since nothing was adjusted for my leg length. I sat frozen to the saddle, one hand desperately clutching the saddle horn and reins while the other hand held my rope. A smile was pasted on my face. I couldn't move I was so scared! One of the reporters suggested I twirl my rope. "You have got to be kidding me!" I groused under my breath. "Okay, I'll keep it simple," I thought, doing a few cowboy butterflies with the rope. My leg or the rope (I really can't say which) accidentally brushed against the back flank of the horse which made him jump and rear! He bolted away from the now fleeing reporters, hitting a full gallop within a few strides. My rope and cowgirl hat flew off in two separate directions, as I white-knuckled the saddle horn with both hands with the reins trapped between my fingers and the saddle horn. I was tossed around like a ragdoll, since I couldn't get my feet in the stirrups and those stirrups were too long anyway! With my once- neat hair now flying and my legs flopping, I bounced in the saddle trying desperately to stay on! The camera kept rolling, taking it all in. As the horse and I circled the arena, I knew I had to think of something quick, because I felt I was going to fall off at any second!

Just as I was ready to "bail", Montie arrived inside the arena and quickly realized what was happening. He swiftly gathered up several crewmembers working on the outskirts of the arena and in the bleachers and yelled instructions to them to circle around the horse to slow it down. They ran from their positions towards the horse, then slowed to a walk as they began to circle and force the stallion to slow to a trot, then a walk. Montie got within reach to grab one of the drooping reins and pulled the stallion's head back to get him to a stop, all the while calmly calling to the stallion "Whoa, boy! Whoa". I was so relieved to have that ride end! I sat motionless, my legs felt like jelly and my heart was pounding in my chest. Several seconds passed as I tried to gather my thoughts and wondered if my legs would support me if I tried to get down. Montie kept trying to encourage me to get down and it did take a few encouragements before I began my descent. Shaking all over, I swung my right leg over the saddle. Montie grabbed me as I almost fell under the now quiet stallion and hauled me to the safety of the hard-packed earth. All I could say was "Thank you" to Montie, as I stood next to him, happy to be in one piece after that insane ride. I could tell he was angry with me for getting on this high-spirited horse or on any horse without him being present, and angry at Linda and everyone else who was in on this "joke". He didn't say anything to anyone, but later and privately we all had our own "conversation" with him. That evening in the hotel Montie prearranged for he and I to meet to watch the interview. He was a bit concerned about what the camera footage of my wild ride would communicate to the public, since I was the spokesperson for the show but clearly didn't know how to ride a horse. We sat before the TV and waited for my "spot" to begin, apprehensive at best. Several minutes into the newscast, the interview came on. Watching how the footage was edited, it almost looked like I deliberately came up with the stunt to encourage ticket sales looking comical by losing my hat and rope while riding a wild horse! Montie looked relieved and I sure felt the same!

My hotel room was neighboring Montie's room. After dinner Thursday night, I relaxed by watching a couple of television shows – which were in English, then I turned off the TV, and went to sleep. Sometime in the early morning, I was awakened by a muffled ringing noise. At first I thought the ringing was coming from my phone and attempted to answer it, but all I heard was dial tone. A muffled man's voice came through the wall as the ringing stopped and the phone was answered. The voice was Montie! I turned on the light to check the clock. Three am! With the walls so paper thin, I had no difficulty listening to the one-sided conversation. I felt guilty listening, but I couldn't help hearing what was being said, especially as his voice became louder due to his frustration over whatever the conversation was about. Best I could figure, it sounded like the Native American Indians in our show had gone to a bar (against Montie's orders), drank too much liquor (also against Montie's orders), started to "whoop-it- up" letting their Indian hair braids down from their hats, and were all arrested for being drunk and the "men wearing long hair in public". Remember, it is against the Singapore law for men to wear long hair unrestricted and Montie had negotiated with the government to have the "Indians" in the show to hide their long braids under their hats. I heard an "I'll be down", the phone replaced in its cradle with a bang, and some rustling movement in the room. After a few minutes, a door opened and closed with footsteps moving towards the elevator. Sleep eluded me, since I began to worry that the Indians would be asked to leave the country, or worse, their hair would be cut short (which was against their religion). Somehow I must have fallen back to sleep, waking when Montie returned to his room about three hours later, banging the door as he entered. I immediately called his room, explaining I had heard his door slam and wondered if he was okay. He explained to me about the phone call he had received from one of the Native Americans and told me the last thing he needed was to have these guys get in trouble. Montie had been informed by the Singapore Officials that had met him at the Police Station that the Indians could do the two weekend shows, and then they would need to leave the country immediately after that last performance. Montie ended our call and I decided since I was awake I might as well get dressed to go down for an early breakfast.

Friday, the opening night for the Wild West Show! Montie disclosed to us that ticket sales were down, because of the forecasted threat of rain. The turnout was poor –no thanks to the intermittent showers that scared off the audience- for all four shows. We performed as always, since it didn't rain hard, just sprinkles with a bit of rain here and there. The show proceeds in Singapore weren't good, so Montie and our sponsors just barely broke even after all of us were paid.

From Singapore we traveled to Bangkok, Thailand, for one weekend of shows. Bangkok was such a neat place to visit, offering a variety of events to enjoy, such as exotic dancers, royal temples, and open-air markets, Siamese boats on the city's multiple waterways, plus other old-world sights and sounds.

98

Chapter 13

Bangkok Experiences, Hong Kong & Home

I didn't have to do any television or newspaper interviews in Bangkok, because there were posters up in most all the hotels and other public venues advertising the show and with that advertisement in place, ticket sales were going well. Since the weather was beautiful and I had "down" time, I decided to hire a rickshaw to take me to the indoor arena and, upon arriving, I quickly noted it was much smaller than the other, much larger sports arena in which we had previously performed. Too bad the weather was not on our side! We sure could have had nice weather in Singapore's open stadium!

That evening Montie took a few of us out to dinner for Thai food. First on the menu was Turtle soup. It was a broth with -yes- a small turtle floating in each bowl of soup. Eww!! Montie spotted my scrunched-up face, making me taste it by helping me scoop a piece of turtle and broth in my spoon, then forcing my hand, spoon, and the disgusting contents to my mouth. It tasted disgusting and I spat it out in my water glass.

After the nasty Turtle soup entree, we were shown to the fish tank near the front of the restaurant to pick out a live fish to cook at our table. I had happened to look into the fish tank when we first came in, spotting a dead fish floating on top of the tank with the live fish swimming glibly around under this corpse. Yuck!! And EWW!! I managed to dodge this Siamese delicacy by filling my plate with as many rice dishes at the table as possible.

Already Thursday and I hadn't had any time for practicing new rope tricks since Malaysia! I also wanted to continue adding new tricks as well, so I set out to try to find my "new roping tricks source" John Brady that morning, finding him in a workout room in the hotel doing pull-ups and sit ups. He always prided himself on being in the best of shape! I poked my head into the exercise room, pleading with him about how much I wanted to really learn to do the "Texas Skip." After he was finished with his workout, we went up to his room where Vi was having her morning tea. John dug around in one of his rope bags, finally locating an old Texas Skip rope, which has a brass Honda to keep open the loop so the performer could complete multiple jumps through the loop. John said I would need this special rope with which to practice and he would let me borrow it until I could find one of my own. We went down to the show arena to the backstage area where he gave me a couple of lessons. John has always been so nice to me, helping me learn new rope tricks! I didn't want to mess up and disappoint him! He showed me the brass Honda of the rope, to let me know never to let that part hit me on the head or face as it can really cut and hurt. At first, John opened the loop on his right side of his body then, began to demonstrate the trick by jumping in and out of it. Wow! I turned to Vi saying, "It looks so easy, but it's not, is it?" John completed his demonstration, handing the rope to me. I smiled, but knew I didn't have a clue how to start the spin, clockwise or counterclockwise. Getting accustomed to the Honda alone was extremely different from regular ropes, which didn't have it. Time and time again I tried to start the loop, which kept flip-flopping either in front or behind me! I was supposed to start the loop, keep it going, AND jump through it! Yeah, r-i-g-h-t!! I decided this is something I just would have to practice...and practice...and practice! I ended up wearing headgear to protect my head from that hard brass Honda, just so I could practice the trick without fear of hurting myself. I did thank John for his generosity, his patience and the lesson, plus the use of his rope.

All our performances that weekend in Bangkok were attended by smaller audiences, but the Siamese people roared, applauded, and cheered with as much enthusiasm as any of our larger groups of spectators! They thoroughly enjoyed our shows.

We boarded the airplane bound for Hong Kong. This would be our last stop on our show tour. This stop was a holiday for us. I enjoyed Hong Kong with all its nightlife and shopping. I found the prices of silk fabrics and the tailors in Hong Kong comparable to the Malaysian prices for fabric and tailors, so I had several more blouses made before our journey home to

America. On Tuesday we boarded the airplane for home, arriving in Los Angeles, California, actually a day before we left! We had crossed the International Date Line, so we were "reliving" a day. It was well after dark when we arrived, everyone scattering to their homes or continuing their flights to their destinations. All the performers were excited to finally be back "home" to be with their loved ones and spend their paychecks, so all took off to their corner of the world. The Bradys, however, stayed in Los Angeles for a few days visiting friends before leaving for home in Sydney, Australia. I was so sad to see this tour end and have to say goodbye to my special friends. Everyone else in the troupe had experienced several tours, so this leave-taking was nothing new to them at all! Montie was visibly relaxed, knowing he would have a few days off until the pressure and stress of planning a new tour was thrust upon him. I had my parents to go home to and was greeted warmly, but I sure didn't want all this excitement to end! I so enjoyed the excitement of the performance arena, the travels, plus new sights that I didn't want to give any of it up! Even with the anguish of certain performers who were mean to me, I still missed the constant "moving"! This was the end of my first tour!

Since Montie had said before our departure from Hong Kong there were no tours lined up in the near future, I had no idea what to plan for next. Would there be more tours?! Did I have to go find a job? Would it need to be permanent? I didn't want to continue to live with my parents, having enjoyed the privacy of being by myself, but now, would I need to find a place of my own? How long would this recess from performing be? Too many questions crashed in my mind as I struggled to figure out my next thing to do.

I did go back to my parents' house to live for a short time, since I had no apartment or house of my own. I had my paycheck from the tour, but it wasn't going to last forever, so I realized I would need to find a job until Montie could contact me about another tour. But... I am "Miss Wild West of the Buffalo Bill's Wild West Show" and Montie had promised I would continue to be with the show. Now all I had to do was wait for Montie to call and tell me of our next new adventure!

Once you get a taste of the cowboy's life it's hard to go back to being an "ordinary" person!

Look for the next Wild West adventure...

"Miss Wild West Goes to Brazil"!

by

Chyrle Bacon